D1222887

The Fifth Profession

Becoming a Psychotherapist

William E. Henry
John H. Sims
S. Lee Spray

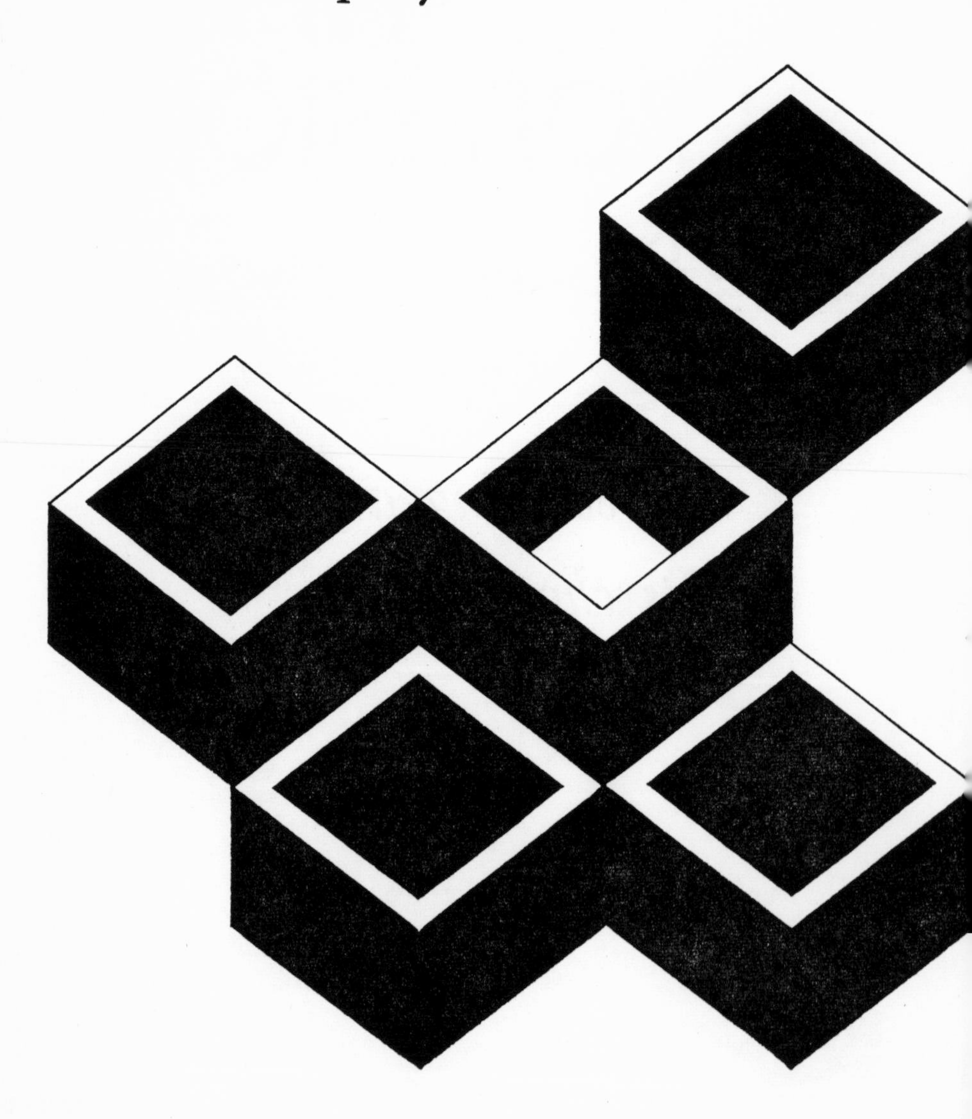

THE FIFTH PROFESSION

Jossey-Bass Inc., Publishers
615 Montgomery Street • San Francisco • 1971

THE FIFTH PROFESSION
Becoming a Psychotherapist
William E. Henry, John H. Sims, and S. Lee Spray

Jossey-Bass, Inc., Publishers
615 Montgomery Street
San Francisco, California 94111

Library of Congress Catalog Card Number 71-148655

International Standard Book Number ISBN 0-87589-088-1

Manufactured in the United States of America
Composed and printed by York Composition Company
Bound by Chas. H. Bohn & Co., Inc.

JACKET DESIGN BY JANE OKA, SAN FRANCISCO

FIRST EDITION

Code 7106

THE JOSSEY-BASS
BEHAVIORAL SCIENCE SERIES

General Editors

WILLIAM E. HENRY, *University of Chicago*

NEVITT SANFORD, *Wright Institute, Berkeley*

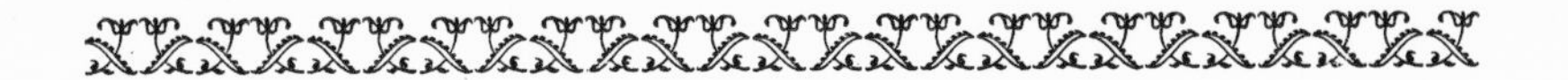

Preface

Four training systems produce psychotherapists—psychiatry, psychoanalysis, social work, psychology. Each of these routes has a manifestly different goal and sees itself as producing not only different but uniquely qualified people. We have attempted to examine, in a study in part reported in *The Fifth Profession,* the ways in which recruits enter these respective systems of training, how they choose and select among the offerings in each system, and how they emerge at the end as psychotherapists. We have been greatly impressed with two factors not at all apparent from the presence of these four training systems. The first is that the entrants into any of these four systems who finally do become psychotherapists are highly similar in social and cultural background. They come from a highly circumscribed sector of the social world, representing a social marginality in ethnic, religious, and political terms. And the second factor is that as each therapist chooses among the offerings in his particular training system, he does so in ways which appear to parallel the choices of his colleagues in other systems. In this process, the members of these systems become again alike in emphasizing particular views and experiences, and each emerges at the end of training with a firm commitment to the psychotherapeutic stance. Members of each group triumph over the manifest goals of their particular training system and become with time increasingly like their colleague psychotherapists in other training systems. The marks of the professional training route which remain upon them seem to reside far more largely in residuals of professional separatism than in views of the patient or in ways of relating to him.

We will later report on the ways in which these similarities in background and in posttraining stance seem to be paralleled in therapy practice. But we already present here quite enough material to raise the question of the social economy of having four different training systems, producing four different groups of professionals in the mental health field, which among them produce a fifth, the psychotherapist.

We express our indebtedness to the many persons who contributed their time and talent to our study: to National Institute of Mental Health, United States Public Health Service, which, through Grant MH-09192, provided financial support; to the experienced professionals who served as initial informants, as distinct from subjects, about persons and processes in the mental health worlds of the areas from which we gathered our main data: Theodora Abel, Francesca Alexander, Jules Barron, Virginia Bellsmith, Hedda Bolgar, Arthur Carr, Catherine Cullinan, Mary Dunkel, David Fanshel, Hyman Forstenzer, Eugene Gendlin, Ernest Greenwood, Robert Holt, Oliver J. B. Kerner, Henry Maas, Robert McFarland, Mortimer Meyer, Helen Perlman, Nathaniel Raskin, Melvin Sabshin, Harold Sampson, Jackson Smith, Fred Spaner, Anselm Strauss, William Thetford, Harold Visotsky, Ruth Weichelbaum, Joseph Wepman; to the colleagues and students who assisted in the collection and analysis of data: Robert Beck, Bernice Bild, Byron Boyd, Richard Ford, Richard Gilman, Harold Kooden, Marylou Lionells, Marc Lubin, John Marx, Harvey Molotch, Joan Neff, Jean Prebis, Elliot Simon, Josh Yeidel; to Estelle Buccino, Alice Chandler, and Hildegarde Sletteland, for their splendid administrative support; and, most importantly, to the more than 4000 mental health professionals who contributed mightily of their time and understanding to help us to understand some portion of the origins and lives of those who devote themselves to the problems of others.

Chicago
December 1970

WILLIAM E. HENRY
JOHN H. SIMS
S. LEE SPRAY

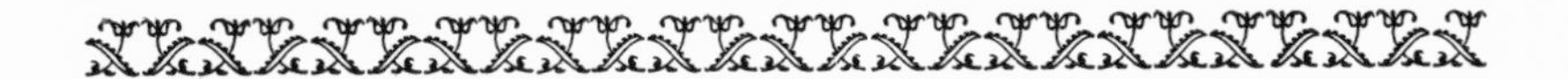

Contents

The Fifth Profession

Becoming a Psychotherapist

I

Emergence of the Fifth Profession

Mental disturbance, whether perceived as a disease or as a problem of living, has been a special problem for modern societies. In some respects analogous to the criminal or the delinquent, the mentally disturbed person has been shunned socially when constituting a minor social inconvenience and has been isolated physically in institutions when the threat he presents to the functioning of society is greater. The incarceration of the mentally ill in hospitals seemed an appropriate solution, especially when the mental disturbance was seen as a form of medical problem or when the disturbance carried with it overtones of moral transgressions. Under these circumstances the training and subsequent practice of the mental health professional focused heavily on care under custodial conditions—a training in which the medical aspects of mental disturbances understandably took a central role.

This domination of the field by concerns of custodial care began to weaken toward the end of the nineteenth century and was replaced, as a focus of training and professional concern, with ideological issues dealing with psychiatric theories and techniques. These new theories, and especially those vigorously stimulated by the introduction of psychoanalysis, provided not only a new set of explanations and techniques but also a rationale for treatment outside institutions. Although it offered some of its own mysteries, psychoanalysis nonetheless provided a set of terms and a logic concerning the development of disturbed behavior that had a certain plausibility and that were vastly preferable to the intimations of moral transgressions and mysterious medical afflictions that characterized the preceding period.

Psychoanalytic thought provided a focus for serious debate among psychiatrists. Its particular vocabulary and rational approach to man's behavior also began to diffuse to the general public. But with the availability of terms of some ordinary nature (mothers and fathers and guilt and social experience), and with a new scientific logic that appealed to one's need for causal explanations, the psychiatric mystique, and mental disturbance itself, began its trek out of the dark realms of magic and mystery and into the broad realms of ordinary, educated social exchange.

As it did, the professionals who were active in the field, and especially the newcomers attracted by the new logic, became embroiled in debate on systems of explanation and on the elaboration of techniques of cure. This debate, although most intense in medical circles, carried over into nonmedical contexts and began to enjoin the interest of other groups whose problems and concerns appeared to have some relevance to it. The psychologist, already concerned with some forms of mental phenomena, began to connect the issues and terms of the psychoanalytic debate to his own concerns, especially when some question of mental distress arose. The worker in welfare and in delinquency and adult crime began to see pertinence to his concerns.

The outbreak of World War II brought to the fore these partially developed interests among a wide range of professional groups. The presence of substantial numbers of mentally disturbed persons not only challenged the available psychiatric facilities but made grossly apparent the notion that these disturbances might be understood and treated in contexts that were not fully medical. Meaningful systems of explanation and treatment existed that neither rested conceptually on medicine nor made an exclusively medical setting necessary for treatment. This combination of circumstances led to the extension of programs of training for psychiatrists and to the introduction of training programs for other professions, notably psychology and social work.

The continued sense of need for mental health services and the seeming success of systems of treatment under the direction of psychologists and social workers encouraged the extension of various forms of treatment training to other fields. The family counselor, the pastoral counselor, the school psychologist, and the guidance counselor are among those with some claim to mental health treatment skills. In more recent years, of course, psychiatrically based techniques have expanded with more common use of drugs, and other techniques have also been aimed at reducing the time involved in the classical one-to-one therapeutic relationship. Group therapy, community psychology, and the community mental health movement generally are all attempts at treating larger numbers of people.

The community mental health movement, however, has two additional goals: providing treatment to persons for whom the usual psychotherapy has seldom been available, in particular the poor, minority groups, and the elderly; and providing services that are more within the context of the normal living circumstances of the persons in need. A third but seldom articulated aim has been that of managing the normal living circumstances (the community) in such a manner as to prevent or reduce the likelihood of serious disturbance.

A related development is the encounter group movement. Although this effort at group experiencing bears some relation to formal group therapy and its therapeutic aims, the movement has had substantial stimulus from outside traditional mental health professionals and has enjoyed the interest of many hundreds of persons for whom the group encounter has no intended mental health or therapeutic aim. In the encounter movement, as well as in the more formal community mental health context, mental health services have come increasingly to be performed by nonprofessionals—that is, by persons with no formal training in these roles and who are in no way members of the core mental health professions: psychoanalysis, psychiatry, clinical psychology, psychiatric social work.

Nevertheless, the core mental health professions still provide the most significant portion of mental health care and serve as the models for training in formal institutions. The individual professional associations that represent these professions also serve as guides to the accreditation of the professionals for practice and take over from training institutions significant aspects of the setting and maintenance of standards.

The competing associations and ideologies that characterized the earliest developments in mental health have continued to serve as rallying points for professional identities and as topics of theoretical debate. The training programs developed for these professions tend to reflect certain basic images of each professional group, and each profession and its related training setting have maintained significant degrees of distance from other professions. The central dividing line has been the commitment to the medical image, as represented in the training for the M.D. degree. Two of the professions with which this book deals, psychiatry and psychoanalysis, formally demand the M.D. Psychiatry represents a specialization beyond the M.D. in what represents mental health care of a medical character. Although there is some debate regarding the amount of general medicine needed before psychiatric specialization, the psychiatric group among the mental health professions represents the clearest case for the utilization of medical concepts. Psychoanalysis is a further specialization beyond psychiatry and beyond the M.D., although psychoanalytic associations have with rarity admitted members with notable qualifications in psychoanalysis but with none in medicine. Psychoanalysts are even further removed from medicine than are psychiatrists. Regardless of the status of the medical aspects in current practice, both psychiatrists and psychoanalysts have had largely overlapping professional training and share in common the intense socialization of the medical years.

The psychologist and the social worker, the other two professions dealt with, have neither the M.D. degree nor its generally concomitant assumptions in medical ideology. These two nonmedical professions also differ from each other, above and beyond their joint difference from the medical groups. The clinical psychologist's Ph.D. presupposes a training orientation to research. The psychiatric social worker, most commonly an M.S.W., has a special training background in social and public welfare that none of the other three professions have.

These are the four professions, each with society's mandate to care for forms of normal distress, with which this book deals. Each of these groups has its own history and its own particular ideologies and heroes. And each has developed its own training format—its own setting for didactic and clinical forms of training. With insignificant exceptions, each training context tends to be exclusive and to provide training and professional experience only for its own members. These facts suggest four quite distinct routes to four distinct end points. Each of these professions also has its own public image, reflecting different properties and seemingly of appeal to different kinds of people.

Insofar as they are relevant to college youths, each of the dominant public images of these professions would appear to attract an initial recruit of different character. The appeal of social ills and of the poor and needy would seem to be different from the appeal of medicine with its biological and scientific aura. And each again is different from the knowledge of inner personal processes implied by the word *psychology*. The choice of these basic fields is a complex of personal motives, of public reputation and image, and of opportunities afforded to an individual. But the choice is indeed made in terms of these background fields and in each profession is made prior to the choice of the particular specialty that led our subjects to the therapeutic aspects of these professions. The implications of these background discipline choices differ. The psychiatrist and psychoanalyst must make the choice very early in order to take the courses that provide the premedical necessities. It is only after the early part of medical training that the choice of a psychiatric direction is made and only after that choice that the additional focus is made on psychoanalysis. The history in the other groups is similar if shorter. The social worker and the psychologist each made his choice leading toward psychotherapy and therapeutic casework after initial work in the parent discipline. These facts suggest that the people whom we here identify as mental health professionals constitute self-selected subgroups. At one level this fact is obvious enough, since all physicians clearly do not become psychiatrists and all social workers or psychologists do not go into therapy training.

For the study of these professional end points, however, the important issue lies in the proposition that the choices made during the professional training of these men and women are all decided so as to emphasize a limited number of elements that come to represent a common core of mental health ideology and practice. Out of these four early professional routes of marked distinctness, based on four populations of students entering at different ages and from different routes and backgrounds, there emerges, at the climax of full professional training, a fifth profession, the psychotherapist. Through the processes of selective choice, of emphasizing certain experiences in particular subparts of professional training, some common threads of personal belief and conviction grow and develop into a remarkably similar set of professional beliefs and orientations as well as habits and viewpoints.

Calling this group of people a profession is perhaps an unjustified use of the term. They have no common professional association, no single journal that represents them all, and no lobby in Washington alert to their privileges. And, in fact, at many levels of action, they are indeed in opposition. Psychiatrists still accuse psychologists of practicing medicine without a license. Social workers in the private practice of psychotherapy still accuse psychiatrists and psychologists of not understanding families or community realities. Psychologists accuse psychiatrists (although not psychoanalysts) of not having had any psychological training—of practicing psychology without a license.

The study of the professions tends, appropriately enough, to stress the extended amount of training given to members of a group and to emphasize the great homogeneity of belief and practice that emerges. High degrees of consensus are observed in identity, in roles characteristic in the profession. Goode (1957) in his article "Community Within a Community: The Profession" excellently illustrates this view, which stresses the sense in which all members of a given profession are alike. A contrary view calls attention to the degree of diversity that does indeed exist if we examine apparent homogeneity within a given profession. Bucher and Strauss (1961) emphasize the extent to which there are actively different segments or loosely organized groups within a profession, each pursuing some common overall aim but doing so in its own way. The material reported in this study presents evidence that both these processes occur. But in each of these approaches the central unit, the profession, is defined as the traditional one, and either homogeneity or heterogeneity within each is observed. In the present study, however, we are calling attention to cross-professional similarities—to homogeneities and uniformities across the four traditional professional mental health groups. It is this grouping of overlapping homogeneities in identity, belief, origin, and practice that we call a fifth profession—a coherence formed by high degrees of common commitment, (regardless of profession of origin) to a psychotherapeutic stance.

One major area of homogeneity may be found in the processes of professional socialization. Although each profession of origin has unique elements and differing emphasis, each requires of all members a distinctive set of skills in social interaction. These are the skills of therapeutic interaction, stressed in various aspects of training and, in varying degrees, in personal analysis or other personal therapeutic experience. These active occurrences are predominant among those our subjects remember and to which they attribute the greatest influence. In contrast, formal didactic training in courses and other nonclinical interaction are assigned only minor roles. These clinical processes are the ones that are the most transforming, requiring as they do practice in skills of social interaction as well as practice in systems of belief and explanation. Through these processes a recruit is transformed into a fully developed professional, and it is these processes that show the greatest similarity across professions. In these processes there is of necessity a certain looseness, allowing for a great deal of purely personal contribution to the socialization experience. This fact creates experiential distinctions among practitioners that do not flow along lines of present professional boundaries. A second area of homogeneity exists in the great similarity among psychotherapists in personal and social background. These two areas of homogeneity—similarities in background and in professional socialization—distinguish psychotherapists in each profession from their nontherapist colleagues.

A major section of the present volume suggests the ways in which experience in training interacts with early background similarities to produce the therapeutic constellation we have suggested.

In brief, our mental health professionals come in highly over-represented numbers from Jewish backgrounds, from urban settings, from parental stock with eastern European ethnic ties. In an important sense these professionals are a culturally homogeneous group but also a culturally marginal one. And in more personal terms, our subjects also share some other characteristics. They tend to have rejected parental political belief systems in favor of more liberal positions. They are religious apostates. And they are socially mobile, a fact describing their occupation but also describing an additional aspect of the separation from the political and religious beliefs of their families.

These attributes of family biography are not related to therapeutic stance merely by coincidence. Not only are they characteristic of large segments of our subjects, they are more completely true of those of our subjects who most clearly claim a devotion to psychotherapy. The greater the involvement in psychotherapeutic activity, regardless of profession of origin, the more these political, religious, and social biographies are characteristic.

In subsequent chapters we shall document and elaborate these various views and findings. In so doing, we are relying on more than 4000 mental health professionals who in a personal interview or in response to a survey instrument provided data on their personal and work lives. The details of our sample and method are given in the Appendix. Here it is perhaps sufficient to report that we interviewed 283 professionals in three urban centers: New York City, Chicago, and Los Angeles. This sample was seen as appropriate for the more intensive interviewing and parallels in important ways the properties of the total universe of subjects and of our larger sample of 3990 professionals who in these same three cities responded to our survey. The survey responses constitute a 60 per cent overall return from the full universe of professionals in the three major centers and may be taken to represent that universe in full.

II

Cultural Origins and the Marginal Perspective

The literature on mental health professionals emphasizes the influence of cultural affiliation in determining entry into the field. Consequently we will begin our examination of the origins of professional personnel in the mental health field by exploring two basic questions: how are mental health professionals distributed among the various cultural groups, and what are some of the important factors associated with affiliation to various cultural traditions? To answer the first question, we will present findings on the relationships between respondents' professional affiliation, cultural affinity, sex, and age. Discussion of the second question will revolve around a consideration of the influence of ancestry, generation in this country, and size of community in which the respondent grew up or current cultural affiliation. The findings not only lend some credence to the popular stereotype of the Jewish psychotherapist but also suggest that, in some respects, the popular image is becoming increasingly more accurate—at least among our sample of professionals.

Cultural Affinity

Mental health professionals in our sample responded to the following questionnaire item: "For you, your spouse, and your parents, indicate whether you or they share a cultural affinity with one of these religious groups, even though there may be no adherence to its religious position: Protestant, Catholic, Jewish, None." (A fifth category, "Other—please specify—" was listed on the questionnaire, but, since only fifty-eight respondents checked this category, it was dropped from consideration.) The responses to this item are contained in Table 1, which shows the relationship between professional affiliation and cultural affinity.

There is indeed a marked tendency for practitioners in the mental health field to have Jewish cultural origins. Moreover, the prevailing stereotype of the Jewish psychotherapist is an apt description of the sample as a whole and is not confined to psychoanalysts. Not only do a majority of mental health professionals in the sample claim a Jewish cultural affinity, but the proportion of practitioners having a Jewish affinity is twice as large as the proportion claiming an affinity with the second most popular tradition, Protestantism. As a result of this pattern, the mental health field is, in terms of professional composition, not only more Jewish than most other professional fields but also much more culturally homogeneous than other fields. Thus cultural affinity may exercise a stronger influence on entry into the mental health professions than is true for most other professions.

Turning to interprofessional comparisons on cultural affinity, the greatest differences exist between psychoanalysts and the other three mental health professions. Specifically, psychoanalysts are much more likely to be Jewish or to claim no cultural affinity and less likely to have either a Protestant or Catholic affinity than is true for the other three professions. Two important generalizations emerge from this pattern. First, as a group, psychoanalysts have a level of occupational-cultural homogeneity far higher than that of any of the other professions. Second, in terms of the background cultural affinity of practitioners, there is little difference between psychiatry, clinical psychology, and psychiatric social work. The likelihood of a practitioner's being Jewish is about the same in each

Table 1. DISTRIBUTION OF PROFESSION BY CULTURAL AFFINITY

Respondent's Cultural Affinity	PROFESSION				
	Psychoanalyst	Psychiatrist	Clinical Psychologist	Psychiatric Social Worker	Total
			Per Cent		
Protestant	16.7	28.7	27.1	29.3	26.3
Catholic	2.6	10.0	9.0	14.2	9.7
Jewish	62.1	50.5	49.8	48.4	51.5
None	18.6	10.8	14.1	8.1	12.5
Total	100.0 (609)	100.0 (701)	100.0 (1389)	100.0 (1106)	100.0 (3805)

No answer = 187
$\chi^2 = 137.40,\ p < .01$

of these professions, and the similarity holds for the other types of cultural affinity as well. In addition, there is no significant difference in the cultural affiliation of males and females in each of these professions. However, among psychoanalysts there is a significant difference in the cultural affiliation of males and females. Specifically, females are more likely to have a Protestant cultural affinity and less likely to have a Jewish affinity than are male psychoanalysts.

Recruitment into psychoanalysis is much more strongly influenced by cultural affiliation than is the case for the other three occupational groups. Thus a major distinction *within* the mental health field is between those trained as psychoanalysts and those trained as psychotherapists. Since psychoanalysts as a group rank highest in occupational prestige and constitute the most professionalized group in the mental health field, we are led to conclude that specialized training has not reduced the influence of traditional social ties, in this case cultural affiliation. Rather, there seems to be a marked congruence between professional identities and cultural traditions.

Urbanism

Other factors, which may be correlated with but not necessarily "caused by" cultural affinity, also seem to play a role in determining who enters the mental health professions. We will examine these issues first with reference to urbanism, measured by the size and complexity of the community in which the individuals spent their childhood years. The questionnaire item was phrased in the following manner: "Where did you spend most of your childhood years?" The alternatives were "Large City, Suburb, Small City, Small Town (nonfarm) and Rural (farm)." For purposes of analysis the categories "Large City" and "Suburb" were combined into a single category, which will be referred to as "Metropolitan Community." The categories "Small Town," "Rural" (nonfarm), and "Rural" (farm) were also combined into a single category, which will be referred to as "Rural Community." Finally, the term "Urban Community" will be used to refer to the "Small City" category of the questionnaire. The data are presented in Table 2.

The overwhelming majority of professionals in each group grew up in large cities. In fact, in terms of the relationship between

Table 2. Distribution of Profession by Size of Community in Which Childhood Spent

Size of Community Where Childhood Spent	PROFESSION				
	Psychoanalyst	Psychiatrist	Clinical Psychologist	Psychiatric Social Worker	Total
			Per Cent		
Metropolitan	73.7	66.8	71.4	65.1	69.1
Urban	13.0	15.3	14.4	16.3	14.9
Rural	13.3	17.9	14.1	18.5	16.0
Total	100.0 (631)	100.0 (726)	99.9 (1456)	99.9 (1150)	100.0 (3963)

No answer = 29

$\chi^2 = 21.898$, $p < .01$

profession and size of childhood community, the major distinction is between metropolitan communities and urban and rural communities. Thus the distribution of childhood backgrounds for members of each of the four professions does not follow the traditional rural-urban continuum. Rather, if mental health professionals do not come from metropolitan communities, they are fully as likely to come from rural as urban communities.

The influence of urbanism on entry into the mental health professions is not, of course, independent of cultural affiliation. The proportion of practitioners in each profession who have metropolitan backgrounds varies markedly among the various categories of cultural affinity. Specifically, in each profession approximately eight out of every ten members with a Jewish cultural affinity grew up in metropolitan communities; the corresponding figure for members with a Protestant cultural affinity is slightly more than four out of ten. Moreover, in three out of four cases there are no significant interprofessional differences in the relationship between cultural affinity and size of childhood community. The one exception is that Catholic psychiatrists are somewhat less likely to have grown up in metropolitan communities and more likely to have spent their childhood in rural communities than is true for the other three professions.

Taken together, these relationships suggest that the pattern of recruitment into the mental health professions is based mainly on the distribution of cultural groups. Level of urbanism exercises little independent influence on the recruitment of mental health practitioners but, instead, reflects the distribution of cultural groups in society. Thus, in terms of ecological patterns, Jews, professionals with no cultural affiliations, and Catholics have two characteristics in common: all three groups are concentrated in metropolitan communities, and all three groups represent definite minorities in metropolitan communities. Conversely, Protestants not only constitute the majority in all types of communities but are also much more likely to be found in rural communities and small cities than is true of the other groups. Hence the observed differences between levels of urbanism are in fact reflections of the available pool of potential recruits for the mental health professions. Specifically, the majority of mental health practitioners come from metropolitan backgrounds because certain large-city minority groups, notably Jews and those claiming no cultural affinity, are overrepresented in metropolitan areas. Similarly, individuals with small-city and rural backgrounds constitute a small proportion of all practitioners because Protestants are both less likely to enter the mental health professions and less concentrated in one type of community than are Jews. In sum, mental health professionals come from metropolitan backgrounds largely as a result of their cultural affinity and not vice versa.

Ethnicity

A second factor closely associated with cultural affinity and bearing directly on the issue of the extent to which psychotherapists are drawn from marginal groups is ethnicity. Clearly, if bicultural experiences and exposure to divergent systems of values are related in any way to becoming a psychotherapist, that relationship should be reflected in ethnic relationships (see Ruesch, 1953). At the very least, an examination of ethnic relationships should provide a basis for further specifying the way in which cultural affiliation influences professional membership. The data on ethnicity come from the following open-ended questionnaire item: "To which country(ies) do you trace your national origins?" The categories of ethnicity used in the analyses were arrived at inductively after first recording all specific responses made to the question by respondents in Chicago, the first community surveyed. As revealed in Table 3, the data provide some support for both of these conclusions.

The contention that mental health practitioners tend to have culturally marginal backgrounds is supported by the finding that, in general, psychotherapists are more likely to have ethnic ties to eastern Europe than to any other single area. Great Britain has the next largest proportion of practitioners, but, for three of the four professions, it is a distant second. In fact, if, on the basis of cultural similarity, Great Britain and the United States are combined, the proportion of professionals thus accounted for still constitutes a definite minority in each profession. On this basis it seems likely that many, if not most, mental health practitioners have been exposed to more than one set of cultural influences. Of course, ethnic in-

Table 3. Distribution of Profession by Ethnicity

Respondent's Ethnicity	PROFESSION				
	Psychoanalyst	Psychiatrist	Clinical Psychologist	Psychiatric Social Worker	Total
			Per Cent		
United States	5.6	6.3	6.2	10.8	7.4
Great Britain, Ireland, and Canada	17.9	23.8	25.7	27.0	24.5
Germany-Austria	19.9	18.0	16.9	16.0	17.4
Western Europe	8.3	9.8	8.9	9.4	9.1
Eastern Europe	48.2	42.0	42.3	36.8	41.6
Total	99.9 (602)	99.9 (693)	100.0 (1387)	100.0 (1055)	100.0 (2737)

No answer = 255

$\chi^2 = 53.886$, $p < .01$

fluence varies according to how distant in time the practitioner is from the source—that is, the question of generation-American-born is crucial to the issue of marginality.

Ethnic patterns not only reflect an important dimension in the social origins of mental health professionals but also provide a basis for further specifying the impact of cultural affinity on professional membership. Thus the vast majority (69 per cent) of Jewish psychotherapists claim eastern European ethnic ties. In fact, the relationship is so pronounced that there are no significant interprofessional differences in the ethnic origins of Jews. Similarly, 58 per cent of the Protestant practitioners claim British origins. Here, however, ethnic origins are less concentrated than is the case for Jews. As a result, interprofessional differences exist among psychiatric social workers, psychoanalysts, and clinical psychologists: social workers are less likely to have British origins than are members of either of the other two professions. Catholics tend to have a slightly broader base of recruitment than Jews and Protestants, with large proportions of practitioners coming from Great Britain (40 per cent) or western Europe (29 per cent). Notable professional differences among Catholics are reflected in the large proportion (49 per cent) of psychiatric social workers tracing their origins to Great Britain (primarily Ireland) and in the greater tendency for psychiatrists to have eastern European backgrounds, compared to the other three professions. Finally, those who claim no cultural affinity are the least specialized in terms of background, with three categories of ethnicity (eastern Europe, Great Britain, and Germany-Austria) containing sizable proportions of practitioners. Here again, no interprofessional differences exist.

The importance of ethnicity as a variable resides more in what it reveals about the origins of cultural affiliations than in its independent influence on recruitment into the mental health professions. Thus the pronounced tendency for practitioners to have eastern European ethnic origins corresponds to the wave of Jews emigrating from this area and settling in metropolitan centers in the United States. Similarly, the sizable proportion of professionals tracing their origins to Great Britain reflects the most prevalent background for Protestants and, to a lesser extent, Catholics. Finally, the distribution of ethnic origins among those claiming no cultural affinity is also consistent with this thesis; the fact that these practitioners come from a variety of different ethnic backgrounds provides further support for the conclusion that ethnicity reflects cultural affiliations. In short, in terms of social background, it is cultural affiliation and not ethnicity that accounts for the major differences among mental health professionals.

Birthplace

Among the variables used to explore the origins of mental health professionals, birthplace is both strategic and unique. It is strategic for several reasons. First, in terms of cultural assimilation and exposure to divergent values, being foreign born epitomizes the marginal position. Therefore, if a bicultural experience is a factor contributing to the decision to become a psychotherapist, it certainly should be reflected in the number of foreign-born practitioners in the mental health professions. Second, native-born persons with foreign-born parents may experience more sharply the influence of cultural marginality than do foreign-born persons. Therefore, to the extent that these influences are related to the process of becoming a psychotherapist, we would expect the mental health professions to have an even larger proportion of second-generation practitioners. Third, since the mental health professions are relatively new occupational specialties, birthplace is an ideal variable to use in assessing the extent to which emerging professions recruit members from marginal groups. Thus birthplace is unique in that it provides a basis for simultaneously examining some of the cultural processes and structural factors that have been found to be important in understanding the origins of mental health professionals.

The factors that make birthplace an important variable all suggest that the proportion of first-generation practitioners in the mental health professions should be sizable. However, the extent to which this conclusion is supported by the data varies markedly by profession.

A sizable proportion of all mental health professionals are foreign born. In fact, to gain some idea of the extent to which first-generation individuals are concentrated in the mental health professions, we need only compare the figures for the four professional groups with comparable figures for foreign-born persons in the general population. Our sample showed that 25 per cent of the psychoanalysts, 24 per cent of the psychiatrists, 13 per cent of the clinical psychologists, and 12 per cent of the psychiatric social workers were foreign born. According to the 1960 U.S. Census, 5.4 per cent of the population was foreign born. The two medical professions have a much larger proportion of first-generation practitioners than either clinical psychology or psychiatric social work. Moreover, the consistency of the medical/nonmedical distinction is maintained even when the relationship between professional affiliation and first-generation status is elaborated by introducing cultural affiliation. Specifically, there is little difference between clinical psychology and psychiatric social work with regard to the cultural affiliations of foreign-born practitioners. Similarly, with the exception of those claiming no cultural affiliation, there is little that distinguishes the distribution of foreign-born psychoanalysts from that of first-generation psychiatrists. In sum, medically trained psychotherapists are more likely to be foreign born than are those psychotherapists without an M.D.

Why are clinical psychologists and psychiatric social workers less likely than psychiatrists and psychoanalysts to be first generation? Since the likelihood of being foreign born increases with age in each of the professions, it is possible that the medical/nonmedical split is, at least partially, a reflection of differences in the age composition of the two groups. Support for this possibility comes from the finding that the two medical groups are older than the two nonmedical professions. However, when the practitioners in each profession were divided at the median point into two age groups, the difference between the two medical groups and the two nonmedical groups persisted, although it was confined mainly to older members of each profession. Thus the profession differences noted earlier cannot be explained solely by the differential age composition of the groups. Similarly, when age and cultural affinity are simultaneously taken into account, the medical/nonmedical distinction persists for each of the categories of cultural affinity, at least among the older members of each profession. Finally, the impact of age on cultural affinity varies so that the only intraprofessional difference in the proportion of foreign born in all four professions is among Jews. Thus, regardless of profession, older Jews are significantly more likely to be foreign born than younger Jews. Similarly, among psychoanalysts and psychiatrists claiming no cultural affinity, the older members are significantly more likely to be foreign born than are their younger colleagues.

Medical/nonmedical differences in the proportion of foreign-born practitioners reflect, to a large extent, the fact that psychiatry and psychoanalysis have a larger proportion of older, foreign-born Jews than is true for clinical psychology or psychiatric social work. First-generation psychiatrists and psychoanalysts with a Jewish cultural affiliation more often entered this country after the age of 20, whereas foreign-born clinical psychologists and psychiatric social workers with similar affiliation entered at an earlier age. The medical/nonmedical split in the proportion of foreign-born practitioners reflects the migration of psychiatrists and psychoanalysts to the United States during the early period when psychotherapy was becoming established as an occupational specialty. Since both clinical psychology and psychiatric social work developed later as specialties, and since opportunities for training were more limited to the United States, these two professions tended to recruit fewer foreign born and those who were recruited tended to be immigrants who had arrived in this country at a relatively early age.

To assess the prevalence of second-generation practitioners in the mental health professions, we confined the analysis to native-born respondents and used birthplace of father as a measure of parental nativity. (Two considerations, in addition to practicality, led to the decision to use birthplace of father as a measure. First, the birthplaces of both parents were, in the vast majority of cases, identical. Second, when a difference did occur in the four professions, it was almost always in the direction of a slightly larger proportion of fathers than mothers being foreign born. Hence the presence of foreign cultural influences in the family is most accurately measured by using birthplace of the father.) The findings reveal that slightly more than half the practitioners in each professional group have foreign-born fathers (60 per cent of psychoanalysts, 51 per cent of psychiatrists, 54 per cent of clinical psychologists, and 51 per cent of psychiatric social workers). (See also Holt and Luborsky, 1958; Hollingshead and Redlich, 1958.) These figures contrast sharply with the much smaller proportion of

Table 4. PROPORTION OF PRACTITIONERS WHO ARE SECOND GENERATION BY PROFESSION AND CULTURAL AFFINITY

Cultural Affinity	Psycho-analyst	Psychia-trist	Clinical Psychol-ogist	Psychiatric Social Worker
	PROFESSION			
	Per Cent and (Base Number)			
Protestant[a]	7.1 (56)	24.0 (121)	17.2 (250)	15.6 (218)
Catholic	63.6 (11)	48.8 (43)	47.4 (97)	41.3 (126)
Jewish	78.1 (151)	75.5 (184)	80.5 (334)	77.5 (289)
None[b]	63.0 (54)	33.3 (60)	50.9 (116)	53.4 (88)

Foreign-born practitioners excluded from the table = 655

No answer = 271

[a] Percentage differences are significant at the .05 level for the following comparisons: psychoanalyst-psychiatrist; psychoanalyst-clinical psychologist; psychoanalyst-social worker.

[b] Percentage differences are significant at the .05 level for the following comparisons: psychoanalyst-psychiatrist; psychiatrist-clinical psychologist, psychiatrist-social worker.

second-generation individuals in the population as a whole. According to the 1960 U.S. Census, 15 per cent of the Caucasian population in the United States had at least one foreign-born parent. Hence the difference between the sample of mental health professionals and the general population is greater for the proportion of second generation in the two groups than for the proportion of first generation. The fact that the proportion of practitioners having foreign-born fathers is much larger than the proportion of practitioners who are themselves immigrants clearly indicates that, in terms of recruitment into the mental health professions, the influence of nativity is reflected mainly at the level of second-generation professionals.

About the same percentage of members in each of the four professional groups have foreign-born fathers. Thus the medical/

Table 5. PROFESSION AND BIRTHPLACE OF Protestant (P), Catholic (C), Jewish (J),

Birthplace of Father	PROFESSION Psychoanalyst P	C	J	None	Psychiatrist P	C	J	None
	Per Cent							
United States	87.1	36.3	18.9	41.2	73.5	34.8	21.2	46.3
Great Britain	2.2	27.3	1.9	2.9	11.5	7.6	0.9	3.0
Germany-Austria	3.3	18.2	10.6	20.6	5.2	6.1	12.8	10.4
Western Europe	5.5	9.1	2.5	6.9	5.2	24.2	0.9	4.5
Eastern Europe	1.1	9.1	66.0	28.4	4.6	27.3	64.2	35.8
Total	(91)	(11)	(359)	(102)	(174)	(66)	(335)	(67)

Protestant: $\chi^2 = 34.90$, $p < .01$
Catholic: $\chi^2 = 30.85$, $p < .01$

nonmedical distinction documented earlier for the distribution of foreign-born practitioners does not hold for the distribution of second-generation practitioners. Not only are clinical psychologists and psychiatric social workers as likely as the medically trained psychotherapists to come from foreign-born parental backgrounds, but as revealed in Table 4, there is no category of cultural affiliation in which both medical professions have a significantly larger proportion of second-generation practitioners than do both nonmedical groups. Thus, in general, the tendency for psychotherapists to be recruited from second-generation backgrounds is influenced much more by cultural affinity than by professional affiliation. In fact, there are only two notable interprofessional differences, and in both cases the contrast is most sharply revealed when psychiatrists are compared with psychoanalysts. The first of these differences stems from the strong tendency for Protestant psychoanalysts to be recruited from old native families. Exactly why psychoanalysts should follow this unique pattern is not entirely clear. However, since Protestants are much less likely to be recruited into psychoanalysis than into any of the other three professional groups, the number of psychoanalysts involved in the pattern is relatively small. Hence it is likely that the distribution of this small number of prac-

FATHER BY CULTURAL AFFINITY OF RESPONDENT

No Cultural Affinity (None)

PROFESSION											
Clinical Psychologist				Psychiatric Social Worker				Total			
P	C	J	None	P	C	J	None	P	C	J	None
Per Cent											
82.5	48.1	19.4	47.8	88.4	58.3	20.0	63.6	83.1	48.8	19.8	48.8
3.6	10.6	1.7	2.7	5.2	15.0	1.8	—	5.5	12.3	1.6	2.3
5.3	6.7	11.0	12.1	1.9	0.8	12.5	7.8	4.0	4.7	11.7	13.1
6.2	19.2	1.4	4.9	4.1	17.5	1.0	3.9	5.3	19.2	1.4	5.1
2.4	15.4	66.5	32.4	0.4	8.3	64.7	24.9	2.1	15.0	65.5	30.6
(338)	(104)	(647)	(182)	(269)	(120)	(501)	(77)	(872)	(301)	(1842)	(428)

Jewish: $\chi^2 = 7.8$, $p =$ n.s.
No cultural affinity: $\chi^2 = 16.28$, $p =$ n.s.

titioners could be strongly affected by discrete events, such as those that occurred during the period when psychoanalysis was becoming formally established in the United States. For example, during the 1920s a sizable number of American psychiatrists went abroad to study psychoanalysis at various European centers (see Lewin and Ross, 1960). Undoubtedly, at least some of these psychiatrists came from Protestant backgrounds. When they completed their psychoanalytic training and joined their foreign-born colleagues in establishing and staffing various psychoanalytic institutes in the United States, the effect was to give Protestant psychoanalysts who had been born in this country the distinctive characteristic of being almost exclusively from old American families.

The second notable interprofessional difference derives from the fact that psychiatrists who claim no cultural affinity are much less likely to have foreign-born fathers than is true for the culturally unaffiliated in the other three occupational groups. To a certain extent this pattern reflects the tendency for the more medically oriented, rather than psychodynamically oriented, psychiatrists to come from old American families (Hollingshead and Redlich, 1958). Although these psychiatrists probably also came originally from the Protestant tradition, they are less likely to be concerned with social and cultural differences and to distinguish between religious adherence and cultural affinity. Hence these psychiatrists may have had native-born fathers but, because of weak ties to cultural traditions and/or the tendency to reject cultural affinity along with religious ties, currently claim no cultural affiliation.

When the findings on nativity are summarized, several generalizations emerge. First, psychotherapists are much more likely to be children of immigrants than to be immigrants themselves. Second, the tendency for psychotherapists to come from second-generation backgrounds is largely unaffected by professional affiliation; that is, each professional group has about the same proportion of second-generation practitioners. Third, the distribution of second-generation psychotherapists tends to vary by cultural affiliation and across professional lines. Thus contained in the data is the suggestion that the proportion of second-generation practitioners in the mental health professions is a reflection of the pattern of differential recruitment of psychotherapists from the various cultural traditions. Therefore the remaining issue is to identify those immigrant groups that constitute the pool from which mental health professionals are recruited. Since there is a marked tendency for second-generation practitioners to claim a Jewish cultural affinity, it comes as no surprise to find that the majority of foreign-born fathers in each profession came to this country from eastern Europe (see Table 5). In fact, the totals for each professional group reveal that slightly more than eight out of ten practitioners have fathers born either in the United States or in eastern Europe. The homogeneity of the population of second-generation practitioners is so great that significant interprofessional differences occur only among those claiming either a Protestant or Catholic cultural affiliation. In both cases the difference is accounted for mainly by the fact that psychiatrists have a larger proportion of foreign-born fathers than is true for the other professions. However, the number of foreign-born fathers is small for both Protestant and Catholic cultural adherents, and both constitute minor exceptions to the general pattern. In sum, the prevalence in the mental health professions of second-generation practitioners from eastern Europe is largely a function of the concentration of Jews in the field and not vice versa. Similarly, the large proportion of second-generation practitioners in the professional field as a whole directly reflects the immigration of eastern European Jews into this country during the period 1880–1920.

Other Factors

Many factors contribute to the strong affinity between adherence to the eastern European Jewish cultural tradition and the vocation of psychotherapy, but they are all undoubtedly associated, either directly or indirectly, with the early secularization of the core beliefs of this ethos. Thus the emphasis on ritual rather than dogma and the strong accent on intellectual understanding—both parts of the cultural tradition of eastern European Jews—made them receptive to an intellectual, nontranscendental approach to understanding human behavior, with the result that they were early attracted to psychotherapy, particularly psychoanalysis. Given this marked affinity between the Jewish cultural tradition and the practice of psychotherapy, it is not surprising to find that the mental health professions can still be characterized as primarily Jewish occupations. However, since the mental health professions have been established occupational specialties for some time, it is surprising to discover that the trend is in the direction of an increased concentration of eastern European Jews in three of the four professions. Thus, when the age distributions of mental health professionals within each of the major dimensions of cultural origins is examined, we find a definite inverse relationship between age and the proportion of practitioners claiming a Jewish cultural affinity. Similarly, the proportion of practitioners having ethnic ties to eastern Europe is also inversely related to age. For both general relationships, psychiatric social workers constitute the only exception. Thus, rather than broadening their base of recruitment, the two medical professions and clinical psychology are becoming increasingly more specialized in terms of the cultural identities of practitioners.

Compared to the natural history of a wide variety of other professions, the pattern of increased homogeneity in the sociocultural origins of mental health professionals is extremely atypical (see Wilensky, 1964). The common pattern, of course, is for an emerging occupational group to broaden its base of recruitment as it becomes an established profession. The reasons why psychiatry and clinical psychology do not follow this pattern lie, in large part, in the relationship of these specialties to their parent profession. Both psychiatry and clinical psychology have developed into distinct and highly visible specialties within the parent professions of medicine and academic psychology, respectively. However, the decision to enter either of these specialties still tends to be a "secondary" choice, made some time after the training requirements for entrance into the professional fields of medicine and psychology have been met. As a result, any change in the sociocultural composition of psychiatrists and clinical psychologists would seem to be based on a correlative change in the composition of members of the parent professions of medicine and academic psychology. Specifically, the increasing concentration of persons with a Jewish cultural affiliation in psychiatry and clinical psychology should be associated with an increasing proportion of Jews entering medicine and psychology. Unfortunately, direct evidence concerning changes in the sociocultural composition of the professions of medicine and psychology is not available. However, there is evidence clearly indicating that until the 1940s there were restrictions, often in the form of quotas, on the number of Jews permitted to enter medical schools (Kessel, 1958; Shapiro, 1948; Goldberg, 1939). It seems safe to assume that the removal of such restrictions would result in an increase in the number of Jews entering medicine, which in turn would result in an increased number of Jews qualified to choose a career in psychiatry. Since persons with a Jewish cultural affiliation are strongly attracted to psychotherapy as a vocation, it is understandable that the proportion of Jews in psychiatry has been increasing over time.

Compared to medicine, psychology has always been more accessible to Jews. That is, there is no evidence to indicate that psychology ever systematically imposed restrictions on the number of Jews admitted to graduate school. Similarly, the educational requirements for gaining admittance to graduate programs in psychology have been lower and less specialized than the requirements for admittance to medical school. Finally, and perhaps most importantly, financial support for graduate education in psychology became readily available after World War II. As a result, psychology became an attractive profession for persons who could not afford medical school. The extent to which this generalization applies to the mental health field is revealed in findings that clearly indicate that psychologists tend to come from lower socioeconomic backgrounds than do physicians. Also, since the socioeconomic background of mental health professionals with a Jewish cultural affiliation tends to be considerably lower than that of professionals with other affiliations, the financial support available in psychology clearly made it an attractive profession for Jews. For all these reasons, it is understandable that the number of persons with a Jewish cultural affiliation entering psychology has been increasing over time. However, clinical psychology did not emerge as a distinct specialty until after World War II. As a result, clinical-psychology training programs have been available in large numbers for only slightly more than two decades. Thus it has been only recently that persons interested in psychotherapy as a vocation could achieve their occupational objectives in psychology. This fact, in combination with the affinity between Jews and the performance of psychotherapy, undoubtedly accounts in large part for the increasing proportion of Jews in clinical psychology.

The third professional group that is becoming increasingly more Jewish—psychoanalysis—differs from the other professions in several important respects. For example, from its inception it has always been a distinct specialty clearly set apart from the medical profession. Similarly, it has always been primarily a Jewish profession with few Protestants and virtually no Catholic members. Consequently, it is not surprising to find that the increase in the proportion of psychonanalysts claiming a Jewish cultural affinity is associated with a commensurate decrease in the percentage of practitioners claiming no cultural affiliation. Exactly why psychoanalysts exhibit this pattern is not clear. However, it is likely that factors both internal and external to the psychoanalytic movement have contributed to this development. Thus, since in several respects the founders and early members of the psychoanalytic movement constituted an embattled minority, it is likely that many of these older psychoanalysts were committed totally and exclusively to the ideology of psychoanalysis and eschewed adherence to any other belief system. However, since it has achieved success as a social movement, psychoanalysis no longer requires total rejection of all other sociocultural beliefs on the part of younger members of the profession. Undoubtedly this trend has been facilitated by the continuance of the public image of psychoanalysis as a predominantly Jewish profession. Finally, increases in the intensity and length of professional training, combined with the continued elaboration of Freudian psychoanalytic theory, have probably increased the significance of cultural affiliation for younger practitioners. That is, these factors have brought about an integration of the personal and professional lives of psychoanalysts, who are thus more likely to acknowledge their cultural affiliation.

III

Social Class Origins and Career Mobility

One basic social attribute shared by psychoanalysts, psychiatrists, clinical psychologists, and psychiatric social workers is high socioeconomic status. This fact is true even though considerable variation in social rank exists among the four professions. Thus, in terms of occupational prestige, psychoanalysts are generally accorded the greatest deference, followed closely by psychiatrists. Psychologists are ranked somewhat higher than social workers, but both are considerably below the rank of the two medical groups (see Hodge, Siegel, and Rossi, 1964; Rettig, Jacobson, and Panamanick, 1958; Zander, Cohen, and Stotland, 1957; Rushing, 1964). However, in terms of objective measures of status, members of all four professions are classified as upper-middle or upper class. One need only examine the figures on income and the amount of education they have received to find support for this assertion. Specifically, the median annual income derived from the practitioner's principal position is $11,000 for a psychiatric social worker, $17,000 for a clinical psychologist, $28,500 for a psychiatrist, and $37,000 for a psychoanalyst. This range contrasts sharply with the median family income for the nation as a whole, reported by the U.S. Census Bureau as $5700 in 1959. The high position of the mental health professions is also indicated by the fact that only 15.5 per cent of all families in the nation received money incomes of $10,000 or more in 1959.

The figures for amount of education received are equally high, with the master's degree of psychiatric social workers constituting the lower extreme and the five to eight years of training beyond the psychiatric residency required of psychoanalysts constituting the upper extreme.

For persons coming from high social class backgrounds the mental health professions can, therefore, be viewed as an appropriate occupational basis for maintaining their class position. For those coming from lower-class backgrounds, entering a mental health profession provides an avenue for upward mobility. The relative importance of these two factors can be assessed by examining the social class origins of mental health practitioners. The data required for such an examination are contained in the first set of figures in Table 6.

Before discussing our substantive findings, a few technical details should be mentioned. First, the measurement of social class origins was accomplished by using the Hollingshead Two Factor Index of Social Position. This index is based on occupation and education, which in this case refer to those of each respondent's father. The Hollingshead Index is based on the separate ranking of occupation and education level. These two separate dimensions are differentially weighted and then combined to get the final class ranking. Unfortunately, the questionnaire item used in the present study necessitated modifying the range of scores for education slightly. Hollingshead specifies seven levels of education. Our scale is identical for the first four levels, ranging from graduate professional training down to high school graduate. Hollingshead lists three categories below the high school graduate, including those with partial high school (scored 5), those with junior high school (scored 6), and those with less than 7 years of school (scored 7). On our questionnaire we had only one category below high school graduate—namely, less than high school. To adjust for this deficiency, we assigned those with less than high school a score of 6, which represents the median point in the three categories listed by Hollingshead. The major discrepancy produced was to reduce the range of class scores from the 11 to 77 stated by Hollingshead to 11 to 73 in the current

Table 6. Profession by Social Class

Total Sample (TS), Foreign Born (FB), Those with Foreign-Born Fathers (FF)

Social Class	Psychoanalyst			Psychiatrist			Clinical Psychologist			Psychiatric Social Worker			Total for Total Sample	Total for those with foreign born fathers
	PROFESSION — Per Cent and (Base Number)													
	TS	FB	FF	TS	FB	FF	TS	FB	FF	TS	FB	FF		
Class I	7.5 (42)	42.9 (42)	43.9 (41)	8.4 (55)	34.5 (55)	42.0 (50)	7.3 (98)	2.4 (98)	33.7 (89)	7.2 (77)	36.4 (77)	43.8 (73)	7.5 (272)	39.9 (253)
Class II	25.8 (144)	27.5 (142)	52.2 (136)	27.3 (178)	32.0 (175)	50.9 (163)	15.6 (210)	20.5 (210)	46.7 (197)	15.3 (164)	13.0 (162)	32.2 (146)	19.2 (696)	45.6 (642)
Class III	29.2 (163)	30.2 (159)	72.2 (155)	24.7 (161)	30.0 (160)	65.6 (151)	26.1 (350)	13.3 (347)	55.4 (332)	23.6 (253)	14.2 (247)	54.3 (230)	25.6 (927)	59.9 (868)
Class IV	35.2 (197)	15.9 (195)	79.4 (189)	35.3 (230)	17.2 (227)	74.9 (219)	44.6 (598)	10.3 (594)	68.6 (558)	45.5 (487)	6.9 (481)	63.1 (447)	41.7 (1512)	69.3 (1413)
Class V	2.3 (13)	23.1 (13)	54.5 (11)	4.2 (27)	18.5 (27)	48.1 (27)	6.4 (86)	7.0 (85)	61.0 (77)	8.4 (90)	6.8 (88)	64.3 (84)	6.0 (216)	60.3 (199)
Total for Total Sample	(559)			(651)			(1342)			(1071)			(3623)	

No answer = 369, 408, 617

For total sample: $\chi^2 = 103.277$, $p < .01$

study. However, we were able to use the same cutting point to define the five classes as those specified by Hollingshead (see also Hollingshead, 1957; Hollingshead and Redlich, 1958).

The scale produces the following five classes, as defined by Hollingshead: *Class I,* "Upper Class," composed of major professionals such as physicians, lawyers, engineers, and architects, most of whom are in private practice; major executives and office holders in large financial, industrial, and manufacturing corporations; *Class II,* "Upper-Middle Class," composed mainly of business managers, proprietors of middle-sized businesses, and salaried professionals, such as teachers, social workers, pharmacists, and accountants; *Class III,* "Intermediate-Middle Class," composed primarily of owners of small business, semiprofessionals, technicians, salaried administrative and clerical personnel, supervisors, and skilled manual workers, all of whom are generally high school graduates; *Class IV,* "Lower-Middle Class," composed primarily of semiskilled manual employees, clerical and sales workers, and small shopkeepers, most of whom attended high school but did not graduate; *Class V,* "Lower Class," composed mainly of unskilled and semiskilled manual workers and low-paid service workers, few of whom completed high school.

We are assuming that mental health professionals currently hold the rank of Class II or above. Since the major distinctions between Classes I and II revolve around such symbolic factors as lineage, residential area, and club memberships, it is not possible for us to distinguish between these two class levels with the available data. Hence the top two classes will be considered as representative of the professionals' current class standing, and practitioners coming from backgrounds of Class III or below will be considered to have been upwardly mobile for one or more class levels.

Examination of our findings in the first set of figures in Table 6 reveals clearly that the dominant pattern in all four professions is one of upward mobility. That is, within each profession the overwhelming majority of practitioners come from middle-class (Class III) or lower backgrounds. More specifically, practitioners in each profession are more likely to come from Class IV backgrounds than from any other single class level. In sum, relatively few mental health professionals were reared in the class level they currently occupy.

Although upward social mobility is a characteristic of all four mental health professions, the rates of mobility are higher among clinical psychologists and psychiatric social workers than among psychoanalysts and psychiatrists. That is, the two medical professions tend to recruit a larger proportion of practitioners from high social class backgrounds than is the case for the two nonmedical professions. Specifically, psychoanalysts and psychiatrists are more likely to come from upper-middle-class backgrounds, whereas psychologists and psychiatric social workers more frequently have lower-middle-class origins. This difference undoubtedly reflects the greater financial burden in acquiring an M.D. degree, compared to a Ph.D. or an M.S.W., and does not imply that psychologists and psychiatric social workers necessarily have a greater concern for status. However, it does suggest that the newer professions of psychiatric social work and clinical psychology constitute important alternatives to medical career routes as avenues for mobility. Thus the two nonmedical professions do not possess the high prestige or rewards of the medical professions, but they do enable persons to move into the upper-middle class.

Individuals who have achieved their present class position largely through their own efforts and abilities have had to overcome a number of social and psychological obstacles. They not only have had to find a way to finance an extended period of education, but they also have had to overcome various counterpressures against mobility emanating from the subcultures in which they grew up. These obstacles seem to be somewhat less serious for men than for women. At least for the mental health professions, males are more likely to be upwardly mobile than females. Thus the class backgrounds of male and female practitioners differ so that, the lower the social class of origin, the larger the proportion of male professionals. This relationship holds for all four professions, with the exception of psychoanalysts from Class V backgrounds. In terms of the social class composition of mental health professions, then, men are more likely to have been recruited from the lower classes than are women practitioners. This fact suggests that male psychotherapists are more likely than females to have experienced the social and psychological stress associated with moving across class lines.

Results thus far suggest that there are not only differential rates of upward mobility among the four professions but also variation in mobility rates of various groups of practitioners within each profession. We have suggested that one source of such variability within a profession resides in the differential ability of various types of respondents to overcome the obstacles inherent in the process of upward mobility. Another source of variability may reside in the differential necessity for various types of respondents to be upwardly mobile. A particular case in point is the foreign-born practitioner in the mental health professions. Although a sizable proportion of our sample of professionals are foreign born (17 per cent), we would not expect these practitioners to come from the lower social classes. Instead, we would expect the national restrictions on immigration, in combination with professional regulations, to restrict the population of foreign-born professionals mainly to persons with high socioeconomic backgrounds. The second set of figures in Table 6 reveals that this is indeed the case.

In each profession, the higher the social class of origin, the larger the proportion of foreign-born respondents. To a certain extent, then, immigration and social mobility tend to be inversely related. Not only are foreign-born practitioners more likely to come from the higher social classes in general, they are strikingly overrepresented among those with Class I backgrounds. In terms of class composition, then, Class I is clearly set apart from the other strata by the disproportionate number of foreign-born practitioners, particularly in the two medical professions.

Although the process of selective immigration strongly influences the distribution of social class backgrounds of first-generation practitioners, it should be much less salient for second-generation professionals. Therefore, from the standpoint of social mobility, it is much more instructive to examine the class backgrounds of second-generation practitioners. This is done in the third set of figures in Table 6.

In terms of social class background, the pattern for second-generation practitioners is exactly the opposite of the pattern for foreign-born professionals. The third set of figures in Table 6 reveals that the lower the social class, the larger the proportion of second-generation practitioners. This is true for Classes I through IV in all four professions, with the exception of psychiatric social workers from Class III backgrounds. Class V represents an exception in that it contains a smaller proportion of second-generation practitioners than is true for some of the higher classes in all professions except psychiatric social work. However, Class V does contain a larger proportion of second-generation practitioners than does Class I in all four professions, and in three of the four professions it contains proportionally more second-generation practitioners than the top two strata. In brief, those who have been upwardly mobile are more likely than the socially stable to be second-generation Americans. This fact is true for all four professions, even though the two medical groups have a larger proportion of second-generation practitioners coming from the top four strata than is the case for the two nonmedical professions. Clinical psychology and psychiatric social work do recruit more practitioners from the lowest strata than is true for the two medical professions, and in both professions the overwhelming majority of these Class V recruits have immigrant fathers. It is undoubtedly easier for persons coming from Class V backgrounds to enter clinical psychology or psychiatric social work than it is for them to become psychiatrists or psychoanalysts. Since the vast majority of upwardly mobile practitioners in all four mental health professions have immigrant fathers, the unique contribution of the two nonmedical professions resides in the fact that they extend this general pattern of recruitment to the lowest class level.

In general, the third set of figures in Table 6 indicates that second-generation practitioners have a high rate of upward mobility. Therefore we can conclude that they have been highly successful in acquiring the financial, social, and psychological resources necessary for completing the lengthy program of education and training characteristic of the mental health professions. However, the findings do not indicate how this difficult task was accomplished. Neither do they indicate who, among the second-generation population, are the upwardly mobile. However, a clue to one possible answer to these questions exists in a finding, reported earlier, concerning the marked tendency for second-generation practitioners in the mental health professions to claim a Jewish cultural affinity. Hence, on the basis of probabilities, we might expect the practitioners who have been upwardly mobile to be predominantly Jewish. In addition, the prediction has theoretical merit when placed in the context of existing social mobility research. Specifically, it has frequently been observed that Jews are both more mobile and more achievement oriented than other religiocultural groups in the United States. Thus Veroff, Field, and Gurin (1962) found that the achievement scores of Jews were generally higher than those of Protestants and Catholics. Similarly, the Jewish family has been found to strongly endorse achievement values in their children (Strodbeck, McDonald, and Rosen, 1957). In terms of mobility, Jews have been found to be more upwardly mobile than gentiles (Fauman, 1958). Jews have also been found to be more strongly committed to what Lenski (1961) terms "the spirit of capitalism" than are Catholics. Finally, at a more general level, the results of the emphasis on mobility and achievement are reflected in the occupational and social class clusterings of Jews relative to other groups in the United States. Thus Glazer (1958) has noted that in several cities Jews are overrepresented in the professions relative to their percentage in the general population. Pope (1966) also reported that Jews were disproportionately concentrated in professional and business positions compared to Catholics and Protestants. In sum, there is ample reason to expect Jews to be overrepresented among mental health professionals who have been upwardly mobile. If this is the case, then Jewish mental health professionals should have a greater rate of upward mobility than non-Jewish practitioners. Our data, presented in Table 7, confirm this expectation for the two medical professions but not for clinical psychology or psychiatric social work. Specifically, Jewish psychiatrists and psychoanalysts are indeed more likely to have been upwardly mobile than is true for their colleagues who either claim a Protestant or Catholic cultural affinity or who deny having any cultural affiliation. In particular, Jewish psychiatrists and psychoanalysts are much more likely than other practitioners to come from Class IV backgrounds.

But although the overwhelming majority of Jewish clinical psychologists and psychiatric social workers come from Classes III and IV backgrounds, the rate of mobility for Jews in these two

Table 7. RESPONDENT'S CULTURAL AFFINITY AND SOCIAL CLASS BY PROFESSION

Psychoanalyst (PA), Psychiatrist (PT), Clinical Psychologist (CP), Psychiatric Social Worker (PSW)

Social Class	Protestant				Catholic				Jewish				None				Total			
	CULTURAL AFFINITY — Per Cent																			
	PA	PT	CP	PSW	PA	PT	CP	PSW	PA	PT	CP	PSW	PA	PT	CP	PSW	PA	PT	CP	PSW
Class I	13.3	12.2	14.2	8.4	14.3	10.0	2.5	6.0	4.2	6.2	3.7	6.3	12.6	6.5	10.5	10.7	7.5	8.3	7.3	7.2
Class II	42.2	32.8	22.2	18.5	14.3	28.3	11.0	6.0	20.0	24.1	13.1	15.6	29.5	29.0	12.7	14.3	25.3	27.5	15.2	14.9
Class III	20.0	21.1	23.7	19.1	28.6	15.0	22.9	22.8	32.2	25.1	27.9	25.7	26.3	40.3	27.1	28.6	29.0	24.5	26.2	23.6
Class IV	22.2	28.3	34.9	43.6	14.3	33.3	46.6	53.7	42.1	42.7	50.5	45.1	29.5	24.2	42.5	44.0	35.8	35.8	44.9	45.9
Class V	2.2	5.6	5.0	10.4	28.5	13.3	16.9	11.4	1.5	1.9	4.8	7.3	2.1	—	7.2	2.4	2.4	3.8	6.3	8.4
Total	(90)	(180)	(338)	(298)	(14)	(60)	(118)	(149)	(335)	(323)	(642)	(494)	(95)	(62)	(181)	(84)	(534)	(625)	(1279)	(1025)

No answer = 104, 109, 187, 129

$\chi^2 = 84.207, 48.866, 92.661, 27.615$

$p < .01$

professions does not exceed that of the other categories of cultural affiliation. In fact, in both professions it is the Catholics who have the smallest proportion of practitioners recruited from Classes I and II. Hence it is the practitioners with a Catholic cultural affinity who are the most likely to have been upwardly mobile in these two professions. It should also be noted that the higher rate of upward mobility among Catholics, compared to Jews, is not accounted for solely by the greater recruitment of the former from Class V backgrounds. Of course, a larger proportion of Catholics do come from the lowest social class than is true for Jews. However, when Classes III and IV are combined, the proportion of Catholics actually exceeds the proportion of Jews coming from these strata in psychiatric social work and is only slightly smaller in clinical psychology. Finally, psychiatric social work is unique among the professions in that those who deny having any cultural affiliation are as likely as Jews to be recruited from Classes III and IV.

When our findings in Table 7 are summarized, several important generalizations emerge. First, it is in the two professions that have the lowest proportions of upwardly mobile practitioners—psychoanalysis and psychiatry—that the Jews have a higher rate of mobility than non-Jews. Apparently the Jewish emphasis on achievement and success is primarily focused on medical careers and reflects recognition of the high prestige of these professions as well as the opportunity for private practice and the remuneration associated with it. Second, Jewish practitioners in all four professions are more likely to be recruited from Class IV backgrounds than from any other single stratum. Undoubtedly this fact reflects the concentration of Jewish immigrants in certain occupational categories, such as shopkeepers, clerical workers, and salesworkers. Nevertheless, this finding has important implications for social mobility. Specifically, it has resulted in the upwardly mobile second-generation Jews being a much more homogeneous group than is true for the religiocultural groups whose composition is more uniformly spread across several class levels and among the occupations within each level. Thus upwardly mobile Jews not only share a cultural tradition but also tend to share a single class culture and set of occupational subcultures to a greater extent than do Protestants or Catholics. Finally, the findings support the generalization that, the lower the social status of the profession, the greater the tendency for practitioners with either a Protestant or Catholic cultural affinity to be recruited from Class IV backgrounds. This is in marked contrast to the Jews, who uniformly come from Class IV backgrounds, and suggests that lower-middle-class Protestants and Catholics are not so committed to a career in the medical professions as are their Jewish counterparts.

Upward social mobility is a dominant biographical characteristic of mental health professionals in general. In an attempt to answer the question of who, among our sample, are the upwardly mobile, we have examined the relationship of cultural affinity to social class background. In general we had expected Jewish mental health professionals to have higher rates of upward mobility than non-Jewish practitioners. This prediction received only partial support from the data. However, other data can be brought to bear on this issue. That is, we have examined the distribution of the various categories of cultural affinity among the five social class levels, but we have not taken into account the fact that the majority of mental health professionals claim a Jewish cultural affiliation. Thus, although the rate of upward mobility may be higher for Catholics than Jews in some professions, it is still possible, given their numerical superiority, for Jews to be overrepresented among mental health professionals who have been upwardly mobile. Stated in this manner, the issue revolves around the composition, in terms of cultural affiliation of practitioners, of the five class levels. Since the focus is on practitioners with a Jewish cultural affiliation, we organized our data to reveal the proportion of the total membership of each particular class background having a Jewish cultural affinity (see Table 8).

The findings clearly reveal that the concentration of Jews in each stratum is inversely related to class level. Specifically, the lower the class level, the greater the proportion of the membership claiming a Jewish cultural affinity. This relationship holds for all except Class V. It also holds, with only one exception, in all four professions. In sum, Jews are overrepresented among the practitioners who have been upwardly mobile. In fact, this tendency is so marked that the majority of practitioners coming from Class IV backgrounds have a Jewish cultural affinity in all professions except psychiatric social work. The deviation by psychiatric social work reflects, at

Table 8. Proportion of Each Social Class Who Have a Jewish Cultural Affinity by Profession

Social Background	PROFESSION: Psychoanalyst	Psychiatrist	Clinical Psychologist	Psychiatric Social Worker	Total
	Per Cent and (Base Number)				
Class I[a]	37.8 (37)	38.5 (52)	25.5 (94)	41.9 (74)	34.6 (257)
Class II	50.8 (132)	45.3 (172)	43.1 (195)	50.3 (153)	46.9 (652)
Class III[b]	69.7 (155)	49.7 (163)	53.4 (335)	52.5 (242)	55.3 (895)
Class IV[c]	73.8 (191)	61.6 (224)	56.0 (574)	47.4 (470)	56.6 (1459)
Class V	38.5 (13)	25.0 (24)	38.3 (81)	41.9 (86)	38.2 (204)

No answer = 525

[a] Percentage difference significant at the .05 level for comparison between psychologist-social worker.

[b] Percentage differences significant at the .05 level for the following comparisons: psychoanalyst-psychiatrist, psychoanalyst-psychologist, psychoanalyst-social worker.

[c] Percentage differences significant at the .05 level for all professional comparisons except psychiatrist-psychologist.

least in part, the relatively recent trend toward the recruitment of Catholic males from working-class backgrounds.

In general, the differences between class levels, revealed in Table 8, are much more pronounced than the differences between the various categories of cultural affinity, presented in Table 7, especially for the two nonmedical professions. However, to a lesser extent, it is true even for the two medical professions, in that practitioners with a Jewish cultural affinity were more likely to be upwardly mobile than those with other cultural affiliations. When placed in the context of the pattern of selective recruitment existing in the mental health professions, this finding becomes understandable. That is, since Jews are more likely to be recruited into the mental health professions than are persons reared in other cultural traditions, the class composition of the professions reflects the concentration of Jews in the lower-middle strata of society. Thus one major reason why Jews are overrepresented among practitioners who have been upwardly mobile is that they are more likely than those with other cultural affiliations to choose a career in one of the mental health professions. At least for clinical psychology and psychiatric social work, it appears that rates of upward mobility for Jewish mental health professions are determined more by occupational choice than by mobility aspirations. This is not to deny the importance of mobility aspirations for Jewish practitioners coming from Classes III, IV, and V backgrounds. The point is simply that, in the two nonmedical professions, Jews are not distinguished from others by their rate of mobility. Instead, the major distinctions revolve around the greater rates of entry into these professions by Jews, compared to those claiming a Protestant or Catholic cultural affinity.

Thus far we have examined the data on respondents' social class background from the perspective of the origins of mental health professionals. However, the findings also contain an important implication concerning current professional practice. Specifically, our findings regarding social mobility raise the possibility that persons who have been upwardly mobile into the mental health professions may also tend to be "overachievers" once they become practitioners. Certainly if the upwardly mobile do place greater emphasis on achievement and success than their nonmobile colleagues, it is plausible to expect this pattern also to prevail in professional practice. In particular, we would expect the upwardly mobile practitioners to place greater emphasis on earning a high income (certainly one important dimension of achievement and success) than do their socially stable colleagues. Accordingly, we have dichotomized the income distributions for each profession at the median and calculated the proportion of practitioners in each class level who are "high" (that is, above the median) on income. The results are presented in Table 9.

In general, our findings support the view that upwardly mobile practitioners are also overachievers, at least in terms of income. That is, in three of the four professions the proportion of practitioners having an income above the median for their profession is larger among individuals coming from Classes III, IV, and V backgrounds than for those coming from Classes I and II backgrounds. This finding is particularly striking when it is noted that the relationship holds not only for the two medical professions but also for psychiatric social work. Having a high income is strongly related to private practice for the two medical professions, and, since upwardly mobile psychiatrists and psychoanalysts tend to become solo practitioners, they also tend to score high on the index of economic success. Upwardly mobile psychiatric social workers are also more likely to go into private practice than are their professional colleagues who have not been mobile. However, since few social workers of any type enter private practice, the observed relationship cannot be accounted for by the higher incomes of private practitioners. Instead, the observed relationship reflects the fact that upwardly mobile psychiatric social workers are more likely to move into highly remunerative organizational positions than are their nonmobile colleagues. Specifically, upwardly mobile social workers are more likely than nonmobile social workers to be administrators and less likely to be psychiatric caseworkers in organizations. Finally, clinical psychologists deviate from the patterns of both medical professionals and psychiatric social workers. That is, upwardly mobile psychologists do not differ from their nonmobile colleagues in their rate of entry into private practice; neither are they any more likely to become organizational administrators. Instead, upwardly mobile clinical psychologists are distinguished by the fact that they tend to

Table 9. Proportion of Practioners High on Income for Each Social Class by Profession

Social Class	Psychoanalyst	Psychiatrist	Clinical Psychologist	Psychiatric Social Worker	Total
	PROFESSION				
	Per Cent and (Base Number)				
Class I[a]	45.7 (35)	41.3 (46)	45.2 (73)	16.4 (61)	36.3 (215)
Class II[b]	47.0 (117)	35.3 (136)	37.6 (178)	14.2 (148)	33.0 (579)
Class III[c]	54.5 (123)	46.1 (128)	38.2 (304)	24.6 (224)	38.1 (779)
Classes IV and V[d]	53.5 (172)	51.0 (200)	39.4 (617)	27.3 (523)	38.4 (1512)

No answer = 907

[a] Percentage differences significant at the .05 level for the following comparisons: psychoanalyst-social worker, psychiatrist-social worker, psychologist-social worker.

[b] Percentage differences significant at the .05 level for the following comparisons: psychoanalyst-social worker, psychiatrist-social worker, psychologist-social worker.

[c] Percentage differences significant at the .05 level for the following comparisons: psychoanalyst-psychologist, psychoanalyst-social worker, psychiatrist-social worker, psychologist-social worker.

[d] Percentage differences significant at the .05 level for the following comparisons: psychoanalyst-psychologist, psychoanalyst-social worker, psychiatrist-psychologist, psychiatrist-social worker, psychologist-social worker.

hold academic positions in educational institutions. Since the income derived from academic positions is not particularly high relative to the income levels associated with other positions held by clinical psychologists, upwardly mobile psychologists do not score high on the index of economic success. However, upwardly mobile clinical psychologists do tend to have more than the median number of publications for their profession. Thus they tend to place greater emphasis on achievement as measured by publications but not as measured by income.

In sum, lower social class origins certainly do not preclude success in the mental health professions. In fact, upward mobility contributes directly to the likelihood of a practitioner exceeding the median income of his profession. Clinical psychology represents the only exception to this generalization. To the extent that income is seen as one index of achievement and success, the upwardly mobile appear to possess these orientations to a greater extent than do their nonmobile colleagues. In short, upwardly mobile practitioners do indeed appear to be overachievers relative to their professional colleagues who have been socially stable.

IV

Religious Biographies: Genesis of Apostasy

A national survey of religious identification in the United States revealed that two-thirds of the population was Protestant, one-fourth Catholic, and only 3 per cent Jewish (U.S. Bureau of the Census, 1958). Although it should come as no surprise to find that the representation of these religious groups in the mental health professions is not directly proportional to their distribution in the general population, the magnitude of the differences is striking. Specifically, 34 per cent of the mental health professionals in our sample are Jewish, 9 per cent are Catholic, 21 per cent are Protestant, and 36 per cent are either atheistic, agnostic, or claim no adherence to any religious position. Thus Jews and those who eschew traditional religious allegiances are markedly overrepresented in the mental health professions, whereas Catholics and Protestants are underrepresented. Moreover, the pattern holds even if the comparison is confined to metropolitan communities, at least with respect to Catholics, Jews, and those who do not adhere to any religion. For example, although New York City has the largest Jewish population in the country, reliable estimates indicate that Jews constitute only one-quarter of the total population of that city (Glazer and Moynihan, 1963). In contrast, Jews total more than one-third of the mental health professionals in our sample. Similarly, one of the few studies reporting on the incidence of religious nonadherence in a metropolitan population (Srole et al., 1962) found that approximately 12 per cent of their sample did not identify with any established religion, in contrast to 36 per cent of the practitioners included in this study. Finally, because Catholics tend to be concentrated in major cities, a comparison of our sample with the national population figures underestimates the extent to which Catholics are underrepresented in the mental health professions (see Glazer and Moynihan, 1963).

The discrepancy between the religious composition of the mental health professions and the distribution of religious groups in the wider society highlights two general issues that constitute the focus of our examination of the religious characteristics of mental health professionals. The first issue involves the extent to which religious ties and occupational affiliations are segregated among members of these highly professionalized groups. In terms of religious identification, it is obvious that recruitment into the mental health professions is highly selective. However, both the extent to which the four professions engage in differential recruitment and the way in which this process operates are in need of clarification. The second issue revolves around the extent to which the nonreligious practitioners in the mental health professions differ from their religious colleagues. The significance of this distinction in religious identification derives from the basic functions and responsibilties of psychotherapists—namely, transmitting and reestablishing commitment to core social norms and values. Since religious beliefs and values form a basic foundation for the cultural traditions of society, the religious position of psychotherapists represents an extremely important dimension for comparing professionals.

Measurement of Religious Position

Mental health professionals in our sample were asked to respond to the following questionnaire item: "For you, your spouse, and your parents, indicate whether there is an adherence to one of the following religious positions: Protestantism, Catholicism, Judaism, None, Agnosticism, Atheism, Other (please specify)." Of the 3992 practitioners who returned the questionnaire, only 130 either specified an "other" religious position or failed to answer the question. Most of these 130 respondents simply ignored the question concerning religious position. Of the other religious positions volunteered, none were suggested by more than three respondents. The first three alternatives represent the major religious groupings, and Atheism, Agnosticism, and None (meaning no adherence to any religious position) represent three different types of departure from traditional religious positions.

It is important to emphasize that it is not possible, using these data, to draw any inferences concerning the relative degree of religiosity represented by these six categories of religious position. Each category represents a qualitatively different position with regard to religion. Thus, just as we cannot assume that Catholic practitioners are more religious than Jewish practitioners, we cannot assume that Atheists are more opposed to religion than Agnostics.* Since the interview did provide data on religious convictions and practices, it is possible to discuss religiosity in the context of the interview sample. These data will be presented later in the chapter.

In terms of the measurement of religious position, one additional limitation should be noted. Our data are cross-sectional, not longitudinal. Therefore we have no direct way of distinguishing practitioners who have adhered to one religious position throughout their lifetime from practitioners who have renounced one religious position and adopted another. Since our interest is in the influence of religious background on entry into the mental health professions, it is particularly important to determine how many of the nonreligious professionals have renounced faith in a major religion and how many had never been religious adherents. To make inferences about the process of professional recruitment, it is also necessary to determine whether the renunciation of religious faith occurs prior to or after entry into the mental health professions. In short, what is required is biographical data. What in fact exists are data consisting of responses to questions focused on a single point in time. However, if we assume that the religious position of the respondent's

* It is possible, however, to use the definition of Atheism as representing a greater substantive departure from religion than Agnosticism, to argue that, in terms of content, Atheism is a more extreme type of nonbelief than is Agnosticism or no religious position. Similarly, in terms of content, Agnosticism represents a greater substantive departure from religious adherence than does None, defined as no specific position regarding religion.

father represents the faith to which the professional was exposed during childhood, then an indirect measure of religious background is available.

By comparing the practitioner's current religious position with that of his father, it is possible to define four types of religious biography. Respondents whose current religious position is one of adherence to either Protestantism, Catholicism, or Judaism and whose parents were of the same faith will be referred to as *Religious Adherents*. The term *Religious Apostate* will be used to refer to respondents who come from a religious background but who currently characterize their religious position as Atheism, Agnosticism, or None. *Secular Adherents* refers to respondents whose own position and that of their parents is Atheism, Agnosticism, or None. Thus neither Religious Apostates nor Secular Adherents currently adhere to any of the three major religious positions; Apostates have renounced a religious background but Secular Adherents have not. Finally, respondents who are currently Protestants, Catholics, or Jews but had parents who were Atheists, Agnostics, or held no position with regard to religion will be referred to as *Religious Converts*. The frequency with which each of these types of religious biography is found among mental health professionals is revealed in Table 10.

It would indeed be surprising if practitioners were uniformly distributed among the four quadrants which define the categories of religious biography, and Table 10 confirms our expectations in this respect. Specifically, Religious Adherents, upper left quadrant, represent 63 per cent of the sample; Religious Apostates, upper right quadrant, constitute 25 per cent; Secular Adherents, lower right quadrant, 11 per cent; and Religious Converts, lower left quadrant, less than 2 per cent. Thus, on numerical grounds alone, three of the four types of religious biography are worthy of further consideration. The one exception, Religious Converts, comprises only 66 respondents and will therefore be excluded from further examination.

In addition to indicating the prevalence of religious adherence, apostasy, and secular adherence among mental health professionals, Table 10 also specifies, to a limited extent, the background of these three types of religious biography. First, the overwhelming majority (87 per cent) of practitioners come from religious family

Table 10. Respondent's Religious Position by Father's Religious Position

Father's Religious Position	RESPONDENT'S RELIGIOUS POSITION						
	Protestant	Catholic	Jewish	None	Agnostic	Atheist	Total
	Per Cent and (Base Number)						
Protestant	91.1 (731)	10.6 (38)	0.2 (3)	21.7 (119)	21.9 (87)	13.8 (54)	27.4 (1032)
Catholic	3.7 (30)	86.0 (307)	0.2 (3)	8.6 (47)	7.5 (30)	4.6 (18)	11.6 (435)
Jewish	1.0 (8)	1.1 (4)	97.5 (1234)	39.8 (218)	41.1 (163)	49.1 (192)	48.4 (1819)
None	2.0 (16)	1.7 (6)	0.2 (2)	23.5 (129)	1.5 (6)	2.6 (10)	4.5 (169)
Agnostic	1.6 (13)	0.6 (2)	1.5 (19)	4.0 (22)	24.2 (96)	8.7 (34)	4.9 (186)
Atheist	0.5 (4)	— —	0.3 (4)	2.4 (13)	3.8 (15)	21.2 (83)	3.2 (119)
Total	99.9 (802)	100.0 (357)	99.9 (1265)	100.0 (548)	100.0 (397)	100.0 (391)	100.0 (3760)

No answer = 232

backgrounds. However, 36 per cent of all practitioners currently do not adhere to one of the three traditional religious positions. Second, 28 per cent of the practitioners who come from religious families subsequently renounced the faith to which they were exposed during childhood for a position that is either indifferent or opposed to traditional religion. More importantly, 70 per cent of all professionals who currently do not adhere to one of the traditional religious positions had religious family backgrounds. Thus religious apostasy is far more prevalent than parentally transmitted nonbelief among mental health professionals. Third, the extent to which Apostates come from Jewish families depends on the type of apostasy. Specifically, although 57 per cent of the Indifferents (those claiming no position with regard to religion) and 58 per cent of the Agnostics had Jewish fathers, the figure for Atheists is 73 per cent. Conversely, when those exposed to Protestantism or Catholicism during childhood later renounce religious faith, they are more likely to turn to Agnosticism or Indifference than to Atheism. Finally, although Apostates and Secular Adherents come from markedly divergent religious backgrounds, these two types of religious biography contain remarkably similar proportions of practitioners who are Atheists, Agnostics, or Indifferents. That is, Atheists constitute 28 per cent of all Apostates and 31 per cent of all Secular Adherents; Agnostics represent 30 per cent of the Apostates and 29 per cent of the Secular Adherents; and 41 per cent of the Apostates and 40 per cent of the Secular Adherents are classified as Indifferent. Since the religious background of Apostates clearly affects the likelihood of a practitioner's currently being an Atheist, Agnostic, or Indifferent, the similarity in the distribution of Secular Adherents and Apostates is perplexing. A partial explanation for this similarity resides in the fact that family background also plays an important role in the transmission of religious views among Secular Adherents. Specifically, three-quarters of the Secular Adherents subscribe to the same specific type of nonbelief as that held by the father. Thus it would appear that the pattern of religious nonbelief established by Religious Apostates is consolidated and maintained by Secular Adherents.

When these findings are summarized, they lead to the conclusion that the specific type of apostasy, as well as that of adherence, is strongly related to parental religious position. Thus the basic distinction among apostates may reside either in the particular religious faith that was renounced by the individual or in the current position adopted following the renunciation. If the first alternative is accepted, then no distinction would be made between Atheism, Agnosticism, and Indifference, and nonreligious practitioners would be grouped according to religious origins. If the second alternative is adopted, then practitioners would be grouped according to their current religious self-designation, and Atheism, Agnosticism, and Indifference would be viewed as qualitatively distinct positions vis à vis religion. The marked tendency for Secular Adherents to describe their current position as identical to that of their fathers suggests that apostasy is not an undifferentiated position but, like adherence, contains important distinctions. To distinguish adherence to a religious position from a "cultural affinity" with a religious group, respondents were asked: "For you, your spouse, and your parents, indicate whether you or they share a cultural affinity with one of these religious groups even though there may be no adherence to its religious position: Protestant, Catholic, Jewish, None, Other (please specify)." There were virtually no "other" cultural affinities specified by our respondents.

As might be expected, slightly more than half of all Apostates indicated an affinity with the Jewish cultural tradition. This finding undoubtedly reflects both the absence of intense religious conviction and the strong emphasis on ethnic identity among Jews. Similarly, the fact that a greater proportion of Apostates have a Protestant cultural affinity (18.6 per cent) than a Catholic affinity (3.9 per cent) is consistent with evidence indicating that the Catholic religious community is more cohesive and binding than the Protestant. For both Protestants and Catholics, however, the adoption of any type of apostasy undoubtedly represents a much greater departure from the traditional religiocultural community than is true for Jews. Given these observations, the fact that nearly one-fifth of all Apostates have a Protestant cultural affinity indicates that apostasy is not simply a residual category of nonreligious Jews. This conclusion receives further support from the fact that one-fourth of all Apostates claim no cultural affinity.

Thus far we have focused on the relationship between cultural affinity and apostasy in general. However, if the categories of apostasy do in fact represent qualitatively different positions concerning religion, then we would expect the three types of apostasy to differ in their relationship to the various cultural traditions. Our data reveal that this is indeed the case. Specifically, Atheists (61.5 per cent) are much more likely to have a Jewish cultural affinity than is true for either Agnostics (52.2 per cent) or Indifferents (43.8 per cent). If Atheists do not identify with the Jewish cultural tradition, they tend to have no cultural affinity (22.5 per cent). Although slightly more than half the Agnostics also identify with the Jewish tradition, this type of apostasy is unique in that it is subscribed to by more respondents claiming a Protestant cultural affinity (23.9 per cent) than by those claiming no affinity (18 per cent). Finally, the Indifferent category, composed of those who have no position with regard to religion, has the most uniform distribution of cultural affiliations of the three types of religious apostasy.

Taken together, these relationships suggest that, in terms of content, the more extreme the apostasy, the narrower the range of cultural affinities associated with it. For example, Atheism is largely derived from those with a Jewish cultural affinity and, to a lesser extent, from those who have no cultural affinity. Agnosticism draws support from the same two cultural traditions but also derives from Protestantism. Indifference is the least specialized category of apostasy in terms of the cultural affinities associated with it; those who have no religious position are much more likely to have no cultural affinity. Both Atheism and Agnosticism, then, seem to be associated with specific religiocultural traditions to a much greater extent than is true of Indifference. Thus, although current religious position is a voluntarily acquired characteristic, the data suggest that extreme types of apostasy are more strongly conditioned by cultural traditions than is true for more moderate types. Taken together, these relationships suggest that the three types of apostasy are not simply minor variations on a major theme of religiosity but, rather, distinct positions representing definite perspectives on religion. Hence throughout the study the classification of Apostates will be in terms of their present position rather than their religious origins.

Professional Affiliation and Religious Biography

Religious positions and, hence, biographies among mental health professionals vary markedly from the distribution of religious positions in the general population. This fact leads to the question of how the religious biographies are distributed within the professional mental health fields. That is, are the various religious biographies uniformly distributed among the four mental health professions, or are some biographies overrepresented in certain professions? If certain religious biographies are differentially associated with specific occupational groups, what professional characteristics account for this affinity? Evidence relevant to both these issues is presented in Table 11.

Perhaps the most important generalization emerging from Table 11 is that Religious Apostates as a group are well represented in all of the mental health professions. Similarly, each of the three specific types of apostasy is well represented in each profession. The identical observation can be made with reference to Secular Adherents. Thus the discrepancy between the religious composition of the mental health professions and the distribution of religious groups in the wider society stems from the fact that all four mental health professions recruit disproportionately from the nonreligious groups.

This is not to deny that important interprofessional differences exist in the distribution of religious biographies. The much larger proportion of Religious Adherents found among psychiatrists and psychiatric social workers clearly distinguishes them from both psychoanalysts and clinical psychologists. Similarly, psychiatrists and social workers have virtually identical proportions of Religious Apostates and Secular Adherents, and in both cases the figure is smaller than that found among analysts and psychologists. Even at the level of specific religious biographies, the greatest contrasts are between these two pairs of professions. Usually the major difference is between psychoanalysts and psychiatric social workers, although in the case of Jewish Adherents the sharpest distinction is between psychologists and psychiatrists. Thus both the prevalence of religious adherence and the patterns of adherence and nonadherence crosscut the medical-nonmedical distinction in the training of psychotherapists. In sum, the findings on the distribution of religious biographies among mental health practitioners clearly indicate that the attributes most closely associated with various types of areligiosity are found most frequently and at about the same rate among analysts and psychologists. Conversely, psychiatrists and social workers tend

Table 11. PROFESSION BY RELIGIOUS BIOGRAPHY

Total Sample (TS), Proportion Male (PM)

Religious Biography	PROFESSION: Psychoanalyst		Psychiatrist		Clinical Psychologist		Psychiatric Social Worker		Total for Total Sample
	Per Cent and (Base Number)								
	TS	PM	TS	PM	TS	PM	TS	PM	
Protestant Adherent	11.2 (66)	69.7	21.1 (139)	88.5	20.9 (279)	66.7	24.1 (247)	27.1	20.3 (731)
Catholic Adherent	2.6 (15)	73.3	8.2 (54)	88.9	8.1 (109)	73.4	12.6 (129)	31.0	8.5 (307)
Jewish Adherent	37.1 (218)	88.5	39.8 (262)	88.9	30.9 (413)	70.0	33.3 (341)	32.8	34.2 (1234)
Indifferent Apostate	13.6 (80)	81.2	7.6 (50)	94.0	11.8 (158)	71.4	9.4 (96)	27.1	10.6 (384)
Agnostic Apostate	9.2 (54)	90.7	8.8 (58)	89.7	7.3 (98)	80.2	6.8 (70)	37.1	7.8 (280)
Atheist Apostate	12.1 (71)	85.9	5.6 (37)	83.8	7.9 (106)	72.8	4.9 (50)	30.0	7.3 (264)
Secular Adherent	14.2 (84)	91.7	8.8 (58)	91.4	13.1 (175)	58.9	8.9 (91)	20.9	11.3 (408)
Total for Total Sample	100.0 (588)		99.9 (658)		100.0 (1338)		100.0 (1024)		100.0 (3608)

No answer = 284, 384

For total sample: $\chi^2 = 173.59$, $p < .01$

to possess the attributes associated with religious adherence in equal proportions.

It is possible that the professional differences in the distribution of religious biographies stem from variations in general social characteristics that affect religious identification. Paramount among any such list of potential social determinants of religious biography is the sex composition of the occupational groups. This issue is particularly salient for mental health professionals because there is wide variation in the sex composition of the four professional groups: 87 per cent of all psychiatrists, 85 per cent of all psychoanalysts, and 69 per cent of all clinical psychologists are male; 71 per cent of all psychiatric social workers are female. In surveys of the general population, women are consistently found to be more involved in religious organizations and more committed to religious values and beliefs than are men. Hence it is important to explore the possibility that interprofessional differences in the distribution of religious biographies are, at least to a certain extent, actually sex differences.

Contrary to expectation, the evidence, presented in the second set of percentages in Table 11, reveals no significant sex differences in the distribution of religious biographies either among psychiatric social workers or among psychiatrists. The only evidence of females being more religious than males is confined to psychoanalysis, in which women are significantly overrepresented among both Protestant and Catholic Adherents. However, in both instances the case bases are small, with only twenty females in the Protestant category and four in the Catholic category. Sex differences also exist within clinical psychology, but they do not reveal women to be more religious than men. Specifically, female clinical psychologists are significantly less likely than males to be Agnostic Apostates but more likely to be Secular Adherents. Clearly, interprofessional differences in the distribution of religious biographies in the mental health professions cannot be accounted for by the differential sex composition of the four occupational groups. Furthermore, other analyses rule out the effects of age and social class origins as well.

The differences within the mental health field in the distribution of religious biographies are probably related to differences in the degree to which certain occupational attributes, common to all four professional groups, obtain in any one of them. By "occupational attributes," we mean professional ideologies (belief systems), training procedures, and nature of work. For example, the four professional groups vary in the amount of education and training required to become a certified practitioner (Lewin and Ross, 1960). They also differ in the kind of socialization experiences aspirants are required to undergo in order to be officially recognized as qualified professional practitioners. That is, the four professions vary in terms of the particular attitudes, values, beliefs, and identifications deemed necessary to maintain professional standards in the performance of core professional functions. Concerning the first point—length of time—the findings on the distribution of religious biographies in the four professions fail to support the interpretation that total length of professional training is consistently related to religious background. Thus psychiatrists and psychiatric social workers differ greatly in the length of required professional training yet are remarkably similar in the distribution of religious biographies. Similarly, the religious biographies of clinical psychologists and psychoanalysts are similar, in spite of the fact that the two groups differ considerably in the length of required professional training. This situation suggests that those aspects of training that may be related to religious adherence and apostasy will revolve around those qualitative aspects of professional socialization emphasized in varying degrees by the four professional groups.

A basic ingredient in the ideological socialization of all psychotherapists is the development of a commitment to some scientific explanation (however hypothetical) of human behavior. In the mental health professions a major technique used to encourage a belief in psychological determinism is the experience of personal psychotherapy. (Of course, the very choice to undergo as intense an experience as that of psychotherapy is indicative of a predisposition to a logic of psychodynamics.) Viewed in this light, receiving psychotherapy has definite implications for practitioners' religious biographies and should be strongly related to them. For example, since a strong commitment to psychological determinism unquestionably contains elements inimical to traditional religious beliefs, the relationships between religious biography and receiving psychotherapy should reflect the special historical disputes between certain religious positions and various theories of personality. In fact, there are grounds for viewing religion and theories of personality (such as the psychoanalytic theory) as alternative belief systems.

Assuming that undergoing psychotherapy reflects and/or results in a stronger commitment to psychological determinism, we would expect it to be most prevalent in those professional groups having the smallest proportion of Religious Adherents. Within each profession we would expect the incidence of psychotherapy to be higher among Secular Adherents and Religious Apostates than among Religious Adherents.

Since the successful completion of a personal analysis is a prerequisite for graduation from an approved psychoanalytic institute, the figures for psychoanalysts are not comparable to those of the other professions. However, the mandatory analysis, in combination with the exclusive reliance on Freudian psychonalytic theory (both, of course, well known to the entrant), means that the level of commitment to psychological determinism is undoubtedly higher among psychoanalysts than among members of any other professional group. Hence the fact that psychoanalysis has a higher proportion of Religious Apostates than does any other profession directly confirms our prediction.

Among the remaining three professions, clinical psychology has the largest proportion of practitioners (75 per cent) receiving psychotherapy. It also has the largest proportion of Religious Apostates. Finally, as in the case of religious apostasy, psychiatrists and psychiatric social workers have the smallest proportion of practitioners receiving psychotherapy (66 per cent for psychiatrists and 64 per cent for social workers). Similarly, as in the case of apostasy, the proportion of practitioners receiving therapy is virtually identical for psychiatrists and social workers, and, in both cases, the figure is much smaller.

With regard to the relationship between religious biography and receiving psychotherapy, the findings indicate that, within each profession, Religious Adherents are less likely to receive psychotherapy than either Religious Apostates or Secular Adherents (see the first set of figures in Table 12). In fact, the dominant pattern within each profession is one in which the Indifferent, Agnostic, and Atheist Apostates each have larger proportions receiving psychotherapy than is true for any type of Religious Adherent. Based on these find-

Table 12. PROPORTION OF PRACTITIONERS WHO RECEIVED PERSONAL PSYCHOTHERAPY AND THOSE WHO RECEIVED IT PRIMARILY FOR PERSONAL REASONS BY RELIGIOUS BIOGRAPHY AND PROFESSION

Total Sample (TS), Primarily for Personal Problems (PP)

Religious Biography	PROFESSION: Psychoanalyst		Psychiatrist		Clinical Psychologist		Psychiatric Social Worker	
	Per Cent and (Base Number)							
	TS	PP	TS	PP	TS	PP	TS	PP
Protestant[a] Adherent	98.4 (64)	22.6 (62)	55.1 (136)	32.9 (73)	64.3 (277)	45.2 (177)	51.8 (247)	70.9 (127)
Catholic[b] Adherent	85.7 (14)	8.3 (12)	41.2 (51)	9.5 (21)	44.4 (108)	38.3 (47)	32.8 (128)	56.1 (41)
Jewish[c] Adherent	97.6 (210)	20.1 (199)	65.6 (259)	38.2 (170)	76.9 (407)	50.6 (308)	73.5 (339)	75.8 (248)
Indifferent[d] Apostate	98.7 (76)	26.7 (75)	77.1 (48)	59.5 (37)	86.6 (157)	58.9 (73)	69.5 (95)	72.6 (62)
Agnostic[e] Apostate	98.0 (51)	28.6 (49)	86.2 (58)	38.8 (49)	77.1 (96)	64.5 (93)	88.6 (70)	73.0 (37)
Atheist[f] Apostate	100.0 (67)	28.4 (67)	81.8 (33)	63.0 (27)	86.8 (106)	59.7 (134)	74.0 (50)	75.4 (65)
Secular[g] Adherent	98.8 (81)	18.7 (80)	78.9 (57)	45.5 (44)	87.4 (174)	54.2 (153)	78.0 (91)	90.0 (73)

No answer = 422, 296

[a] Percentage differences significant at the .05 level for the following comparisons: total sample—psychoanalyst-psychiatrist, psychoanalyst-psychologist, psychoanalyst-social worker, psychiatrist-social worker, psychologist-social worker; primarily for personal problems—psychoanalyst-psychologist, psychoanalyst-social worker, psychiatrist-social worker, psychologist-social worker.

[b] Percentage differences significant for the following comparisons: total sample—psychoanalyst-psychiatrist, psychoanalyst-psychologist, pychoanalyst-social worker; primarily for personal problems—psychoanalyst-psychologist, psychoanalyst-social worker, psychiatrist-psychologist, psychiatrist-social worker, psychologist-social worker.

[c] Percentage differences significant for all interprofessional comparisons.

[d] Percentage differences significant for the following comparisons: total sample—psychoanalyst-psychiatrist, psychoanalyst-psychologist, psychoanalyst-social worker, psychiatrist-psychologist, psychologist-social worker; primarily for personal problems—psychoanalyst-psychiatrist, psychoanalyst-psychologist, psychoanalyst-social worker, psychiatrist-social worker, psychologist-social worker.

[e] Percentage differences significant for the following comparisons: total sample—psychoanalyst-psychiatrist, psychoanalyst-psychologist; primarily for personal problems—psychoanalyst-psychologist, psychoanalyst-social worker, psychiatrist-psychologist, psychiatrist-social worker.

[f] Percentage differences significant for psychoanalyst-social worker (total sample); for psychoanalyst-psychiatrist, psychoanalyst-psychologist, psychoanalyst-social worker, psychologist-social worker (primarily for personal problems).

[g] Percentage differences significant for psychoanalyst-psychiatrist and psychoanalyst-social worker (total sample); for psychoanalyst-psychiatrist, psychoanalyst-psychologist, psychoanalyst-social worker, psychologist-social worker (primarily for personal problems).

ings, the argument that religious convictions and psychological determinism are incompatible perspectives appears convincing. If note is taken of the differences between Protestant, Catholic, and Jewish Adherents, the argument becomes compelling. Specifically, the practitioners least likely to undergo psychotherapy in all professions are those who adhere to Catholicism, the religion most strongly opposed to psychological determinism. Indeed, the Catholic Church has its own formally stated doctrine regarding the "cure of souls," and it contrasts sharply with personality theory. The religious beliefs of Protestants, like those of Catholics, contain areas of inevitable conflict with psychological determinism, particularly with reference to the doctrine of free will and individual moral responsibility. However, the liberal Protestant denominations have been much less dogmatic than the Catholic Church in their opposition to personality theory. As a result, Protestant mental health professionals are much more likely to undergo psychotherapy than are their Catholic colleagues. Finally, among religious adherents, it is the Jews who are most likely to receive personal therapy. This fact is consistent with the emphasis on ethnic and cultural traditions in Judaism and with the relative lack of concern, compared to the other two religions, with religious doctrine and dogma.

Insofar as undergoing therapy is the result of a belief in psychological determinism, it should be associated with pretherapeutic areligiosity and hence be as prevalent among Secular Adherents as among Apostates. On the other hand, if the process of undergoing psychotherapy initiates a strong commitment to psychological explanations of behavior, thereby weakening religious convictions, then it should be more prevalent among Apostates than among Secular Adherents. Our findings contained in the first set of figures in Table 12 clearly support the first alternative: within each profession Secular Adherents receive psychotherapy at the same rate as Apostates. Apparently the decision to undergo psychotherapy is facilitated by the lack of religious convictions, even among mental health professionals. Additional support for the view that areligiosity leads to rather than results from personal psychotherapy is contained in an investigation of the mean age of practitioner's first experience in therapy. Specifically, the mean age of practitioners at the beginning of the first experience in therapy is well into adulthood for each type of religious biography (the range is from 28.94 years for Atheist Apostates to 32.16 years for Protestant Adherents). Since the age is well past the period of youthful rebellion and even after the age of occupational choice, it appears highly unlikely that Apostates waited until they entered therapy to renounce their religious beliefs.

Thus far the findings suggest that rejection of religious explanations of human behavior contributes to both the initial choice of a career in the mental health professions and to the decision to undergo personal psychotherapy, because both represent, in varying degrees, a commitment to a scientific model of human behavior. Hence examination of the principal reason for receiving psychotherapy should help clarify the relationship between religious biography and professional affiliation.

Mental health professionals undergo psychotherapy for a variety of reasons. At the most general level, however, the reasons can be subsumed under three (admittedly crude) categories: principally for personal problems, principally for training purposes, and more or less equally for both reasons. The first of these categories is of special importance in terms of our present focus on religious biographies. Insofar as undergoing therapy for personal problems represents a choice of belief systems—traditional religion versus psychological determinism—it seems reasonable to expect a disproportionate number of Apostates to give this reason for receiving psychotherapy. Hence from this view Apostates not only subscribe to psychological determinism as a professional perspective but also experience it at the level of personal commitment. That is, by stating that they received psychotherapy primarily for personal problems, Apostates and others are indicating that they accept personality theory not only as a part of the professional skill system but also as a mechanism of self-analysis. The findings relevant to this general issue are presented in the second set of figures in Table 12.

With regard to comparisons among religious biographies, our findings in the second set of figures in Table 12 are reassuring. Within each profession Apostates as a group are more likely to receive psychotherapy for personal problems than are Adherents. Moreover, within each profession there is a remarkably uniform pattern in which each type of religious apostate is more likely to receive therapy primarily for personal problems than is any type of religious adherent. In fact, there is only one exception to this relationship—namely, psychiatric social workers who are Jewish Adherents. Finally, consistent differences, in the expected direction, also exist among the three types of religious adherents. That is, when the three types of religious adherents are ranked according to the proportion of members receiving therapy primarily for personal problems, Jews are higher and Catholics lower than Protestants. In sum, the fewer the religious restrictions placed on accepting psychological determinism, the greater the likelihood that a practitioner will enter psychotherapy for personal reasons. To a limited extent, this proposition also holds for comparisons among the three types of apostasy. Specifically, within each profession, Indifferent Apostates are less likely to receive therapy for personal problems than are Agnostic or Atheist Apostates. If we assume that agnosticisim and atheism both represent positions further removed from religious adherence than does indifference, then we can view the finding as being consistent with our proposition: Agnostic and Atheist Apostates experience fewer religious restrictions than Indifferent Apostates and hence are more likely to undergo psychotherapy for personal problems.

We have thus far demonstrated that the various religious biographies are differentially related to a range of professional characteristics. Our explanation of these differences has relied on the argument that strong commitment to psychological determinism conflicts with strong religious commitment. Although empirical support has been presented for the relationships between psychological determinism and type of religious *position,* it has not been possible within the confines of the questionnaire data to explore the relationship between commitment to psychological determinism and degree of religious *commitment.* Fortunately, two interview questions did provide data on religiosity that enable us to explore the relationship between membership in the various mental health professions and religious convictions and practices.

During the course of the interview, mental health professionals were asked the following two-part question: "How would you describe your parents' religious viewpoint? What influence has it had on your own religious position?" In responding to the latter part of this question, the respondents characterized their present religious attitudes and behaviors; thus our measure of religiosity deals with two distinct subjects and time periods. Using the same dimensions, it contrasts the parental position defining the religious context in which the respondent grew up with the respondent's current position on religious matters. For parents, religiosity was divided into three separate dimensions: their observance of religious practices and rituals, their religious convictions (belief in a supreme being), and the religious education provided their children. Respondents' current religious position was measured along only the first two dimensions. In each case, however, scores on the separate dimensions were summed to provide an index of overall religiosity. As a result, three groups were distinguished for both parents and respondents: religiously committed individuals, who are intense in their convictions, strict in their observances, and provide religious instruction for their children; church- or temple-goers, for whom religion is both a less intense and less pervasive factor—something for Sundays or Friday nights and Saturday mornings; and nonreligious individuals, who are either avowedly agnostic/atheistic or who consider religion peripheral and irrelevant.

If, as was suggested earlier, the professional differences in the religious composition of the four mental health professions are based on selective recruitment, we would expect interprofessional differences in parental religiosity. The data necessary to evaluate this prediction are contained in Table 13, which shows the interprofessional differences (separately for respondents with Protestant, Catholic, and Jewish cultural affinity) on the three dimensions of parental religiosity. Data on the summary index of overall religiosity are also included.

Our data on this subject reveal four major findings. First, for respondents of Jewish background, there are no interprofessional differences in regard to any dimension of parental religiosity. How lax or strict one's parents were in observing religious practices, how profound were their religious convictions, whether or not they provided religious instruction—none of these factors are related to membership for Jews in any one of the four mental health professions. Second, if a practitioner comes from either a Protestant or a Catholic background, interprofessional differences occur on each dimension of parental religiosity. Third, those interprofessional differences are the same for professionals of either Protestant or Catholic background. Fourth, in each case the interprofessional differences contrast social workers with psychoanalysts, psychiatrists, and psychologists, and in each case the direction of the difference is the greater parental religiosity of social workers.

Given the small numbers in the categories, especially in the case of practitioners with a Catholic background, the strength and consistency of these findings are striking and correspondingly important to explore.

Why should interprofessional differences in parental religiosity occur for practitioners of Protestant and Catholic backgrounds but not for practitioners of Jewish origins? Because, simply put, Jews are Jews regardless of their religiosity. Their identity is primarily cultural rather than religious, and it is that identity that exerts the greater influence on their children. Thus, although there are indeed differences among Jewish parents in terms of religiosity, those differences are dwarfed by the overwhelming and constant importance of cultural Jewishness. Hence they fail to exercise any influence on professional choice. The situation is quite the reverse for Protestants and Catholics. For these groups the cultural identities associated with the two denominations are of lesser importance to their children than the degree of religious fervor that may accompany either.

A second, related question is why the same interprofessional differences are found among practitioners of both Protestant and Catholic origins. Again the answer appears to be the relative unimportance of the cultural identities associated with the two denominations. The interprofessional differences shown in Table 13 are related to strength, not kind, of parental religiosity.

In sum, then, for practitioners of Jewish origins, differences in parental religiosity are unimportant in terms of professional membership. For practitioners of either Protestant or Catholic origins, differences in strength of parental religiosity are related to particular professional membership, but cultural-denominational differences are not. This is not to say, of course, that Protestant-Catholic denominational background differences are not related to different

Table 13. Parental Religiosity: Practices, Convictions and Instruction of Children

A: OBSERVANCE OF RELIGIOUS PRACTICES

Code	*Protestant Origins*		*Catholic Origins*		*Jewish Origins*
	Psychoanalyst Psychiatrist Psychologist	Social Worker	Psychoanalyst Psychiatrist Psychologist	Social Worker	No differences
	(N = 71)		(N = 26)		(N = 156)
	Per Cent				
None	18	—	11	—	25
Light	43	23	37	—	44
Strict	39	77	52	100	31
Total	100 (49)	100 (22)	100 (19)	100 (7)	100 (156)

B: RELIGIOUS CONVICTIONS

Code	*Protestant Origins*		*Catholic Origins*		*Jewish Origins*
	(N = 64)		(N = 24)		(N = 144)
None	37	5	24	—	49
Weak	21	28	29	14	27
Strong	42	67	47	86	24
Total	100 (43)	100 (21)	100 (17)	100 (7)	100 (144)

Table 13. Parental Religiosity: Practices, Convictions and Instruction of Children (cont.)

C: RELIGIOUS INSTRUCTION FOR CHILDREN

Code	*Protestant Origins* Psychoanalyst Psychiatrist Psychologist	Social Worker	*Catholic Origins* Psychoanalyst Psychiatrist Psychologist	Social Worker	*Jewish Origins* No differences
	(N = 62)		(N = 24)		(N = 115)
	Per Cent				
No	22	—	29	14	23
Yes	78	100	71	86	77
Total	100	100	100	100	100
	(41)	(21)	(17)	(7)	(115)

D: OVERALL RELIGIOSITY

Code	*Protestant Origins* Psychoanalyst Psychiatrist Psychologist	Social Worker	*Catholic Origins* Psychoanalyst Psychiatrist Psychologist	Social Worker	*Jewish Origins* No differences
	(N = 70)		(N = 26)		(N = 145)
Nonreligious	15	—	11	—	21
Church/Temple Goer	56	27	58	14	57
Committed	29	73	31	86	22
Total	100	100	100	100	100
	(48)	(22)	(19)	(7)	(145)

rates of entrance into the mental health professions in general. Such differences in turn may reflect general differences in strength of religiosity between Catholics and Protestants.

The final question raised by our data presented in Table 13 concerns the specific interprofessional differences found: the parents of social workers of Protestant and Catholic origins are more religious than those of psychoanalysts, psychiatrists, and psychologists of similar religiocultural backgrounds. Why should this be so?

Before confronting this question, other data should be presented. Table 14 shows interprofessional differences (separately for practitioners of Protestant, Catholic, and Jewish backgrounds) on two dimensions of practitioners' current religious position—observance of ritual and degree of conviction. Data on the summary variable of overall religiosity are also presented, as are data on church/temple membership. As was the case for parental religiosity, the major findings concerning the current religiosity of practitioners are clearly discernible. First, interprofessional differences exist on each dimension of personal religiosity for practitioners drawn from either Protestant or Catholic cultural backgrounds. Moreover, the interprofessional distinctions are the same for practitioners of both Protestant and Catholic backgrounds. Third, in each case the professional distinction contrasts social workers and psychiatrists with psychoanalysts and psychologists, and in each case the direction of this difference is the greater religiosity of social workers and psychiatrists. Finally, although of lesser strength and rarer occurrence, professional differences exist among practitioners of Jewish origin. They contrast psychiatrists with the other three professional groups, and the direction of the difference is the greater religiosity of psychiatrists.

Beyond the overwhelming fact that practitioners, across the board, are far less religious than their parents, two differences between parental religiosity and practitioners' religiosity should be noted: in the first case, the greater religiosity of parents of Protestant and Catholic social workers was contrasted with that of the parents of all three other groups of mental health professionals; in the second case, the relatively greater religiosity of social workers themselves again stands out, but now in contrast with psychoanalysts and psychologists only. Psychiatrists have joined social workers.

Whereas there were no interprofessional differences in terms of parental religiosity for practitioners of Jewish origin, such distinctions do exist on current religiosity of practitioners with Jewish backgrounds. Again, it is psychiatrists who have moved; they differentiate themselves from psychoanalysts, psychologists, and social workers by their relatively greater religiosity.

Juxtaposing the two sets of findings on religiosity, the following questions may be posed: Why do social workers of Protestant and Catholic origins have parents who are more religious than those of the other three groups of mental health professionals of similar origins? Why are social workers and psychiatrists (of Protestant and Catholic origins) more religious than psychoanalysts and psychologists of similar origins? Why are psychiatrists of Jewish origin more religious than the other three groups of professionals who share the Jewish background?

On the basis of our discussion thus far, we are led to conclude that these specific findings result from the intricate interplay of two factors: the transmission of religious beliefs from parent to child and the differing environments provided such religious beliefs by the various mental health professions in terms of their professionalization processes and ideologies.

The explanation of how the first of these factors generally works can be stated briefly and simply: the greater the religiosity of the parents, the greater the religiosity of their children.

The second, environmental factor has been explained by a commitment to some logic of psychodynamics. However, the professions vary considerably with regard to the emphasis placed on psychological determinism as measured by undergoing personal psychotherapy: the order is psychoanalysis, clinical psychology, psychiatry, and psychiatric social work. Thus, to the extent that belief in psychological determinism conflicts with religious convictions, the profession of social work would provide the most receptive environment for those with strong religious commitments, followed, in order, by psychiatry, clinical psychology, and psychoanalysis.

Having earlier demonstrated that psychological determinism is positively associated with religious apostasy we are now arguing that commitment to personality theory is negatively related to religiosity. Support for this assertion is achieved by placing the find-

Table 14. RESPONDENT RELIGIOSITY: PRACTICES AND CONVICTIONS

A: OBSERVANCE OF RELIGIOUS PRACTICES

Code	*Protestant Origins* (N = 68)		*Catholic Origins* (N = 23)		*Jewish Origins* (N = 135)
	Psychoanalyst Psychologist	Psychiatrist Social Worker	Psychoanalyst Psychologist	Psychiatrist Social Worker	No differences
	Per Cent				
None	74	61	73	33	75
Light	19	15	18	17	13
Strict	7	24	9	50	12
Total	100	100	100	100	100
	(27)	(41)	(11)	(12)	(135)

B: RELIGIOUS CONVICTIONS

Code	*Protestant Origins* (N = 63)		*Catholic Origins* (N = 21)		*Jewish Origins* (N = 130)	
	Psychoanalyst Psychologist	Psychiatrist Social Worker	Psychoanalyst Psychologist	Psychiatrist Social Worker	Psychiatrist	Psychoanalyst Psychologist Social Worker
	Per Cent					
None	81	57	89	25	62	90
Weak	12	27	11	33	17	8
Strong	7	16	—	42	21	2
Total	100	100	100	100	100	100
	(26)	(37)	(9)	(12)	(24)	(106)

Table 14. RESPONDENT RELIGIOSITY: PRACTICES AND CONVICTIONS (Cont.)

C: OVERALL RELIGIOSITY

Code	*Protestant Origins* (N = 66)		*Catholic Origins* (N = 24)		*Jewish Origins* (N = 131)	
	Psychoanalyst Psychologist	Psychiatrist Social Worker	Psychoanalyst Psychologist	Psychiatrist Social Worker	Psychiatrist	Psychoanalyst Psychologist Social Worker
	Per Cent					
Nonreligious	74	44	82	31	56	77
Church/Temple Goer	19	33	18	15	28	18
Committed	7	23	—	54	16	5
Total	100	100	100	100	100	100
	(27)	(39)	(11)	(13)	(25)	(106)

D: CHURCH/TEMPLE AFFILIATION

Code	*Protestant Origins* (N = 66)		*Catholic Origins* (N = 21)		*Jewish Origins* (N = 128)
	Psychoanalyst Psychologist	Psychiatrist Social Worker	Psychoanalyst Psychologist	Psychiatrist Social Worker	No differences
	Per Cent				
No	81	62	73	30	83
Yes	19	38	27	70	17
Total	100	100	100	100	100
	(27)	(39)	(11)	(10)	(128)

ings concerning religiosity in the context of the two factors outlined above. The first such finding is that social workers of Protestant and Catholic origins have parents who are more religious than those of the other three groups of professionals with similar origins. From the proposition that the more religious the parents, the more religious the children, it follows that, among the potential candidates for all four mental health professions, some are more religious than others. The point to be explained, then, is why should those who are more religious choose to enter social work rather than psychoanalysis, psychiatry, or psychology? Our explanation is that the socialization experiences of social work aspirants place fewer restrictions on holding religious beliefs than is the case in the other three professions. Since the socialization process undergone by social workers is effectively summarized in a professional ideology well known to the general public, it is clear that this factor would be a strong determinant of occupational recruitment. Finally, the content of this professional ideology revolves around two traditional missions—helping those excluded from or wronged by the social system and working for social reform—that are visibly congruent with traditional religious activities.

Social workers of Protestant and Catholic origins continue in later life (along with psychiatrists) to be more religious than psychoanalysts and clinical psychologists with similar backgrounds. Obviously the above argument remains relevant; that is, social workers began as more religious in that the profession's "good-works" image selected out from the population of candidates those with greater religiosity. Furthermore, although social work's training in causal theory (generally almost exclusively psychoanalytic) constitutes a powerful counterforce, the profession's service ethos and training experience are aspects of professionalization that remain harmonious with religious convictions.

Social workers are joined in their relatively greater religiosity by psychiatrists for two reasons—one similar and one different. Potential candidates for psychiatry are no more religious than those who enter psychoanalysis or clinical psychology, but psychiatry's weaker emphasis on psychological determinism, as summarized in its ethos of treatment and service, is more compatible with religious values than are the intellectual values embodied in the training programs of psychoanalysis and clinical psychology. Secondly, psychiatry's teaching of causal belief systems is far less exclusively psychoanalytic than that of psychoanalysis or, indeed, social work and far less scientific than that of psychology—thus less antithetical to religious beliefs.

These same arguments apply to psychiatrists of Jewish origin and thus account for their greater religiosity as compared to psychoanalysts, clinical psychologists, and social workers of similar ethnic origins. The fact that Jewish social workers do not share the relatively greater religiosity of Jewish psychiatrists is explained by the fact that social work candidates of Jewish background are no more religious than those persons of Jewish origin who eventually enter the other mental health professions. Thus this factor does not (as was the case with those with Protestant and Catholic backgrounds) counterbalance the impact of their training.

V

Political Biographies: Genesis of Liberalism

Typically, political orientation tends to be determined by a number of factors, including social class, occupation, religion, and ethnic and regional affiliations. Insofar as mental health professionals have high socioeconomic status and are involved with a middle- and upper-middle-class clientele, one might expect a predominantly conservative political outlook. However, studies of the political orientations of psychiatrists indicate that they tend to be politically liberal as a group (Klerman et al., 1960; Holt and Luborsky, 1958; Livingston and Zimet, 1965). We also found psychiatrists to be predominantly liberal. Our measure of political orientation comes from responses to the following questionnaire item: "How would you characterize the political orientation of yourself, your spouse, and your parents?" The response categories were: "Strong Liberal, Moderate Liberal, Moderate Conservative, Strong Conservative, None, Other (please specify)." Of the 3992 mental health professionals who returned the questionnaire, only fifty-five refused to answer the question on political orientation. Among those who did answer the question, twenty-five checked "None" and forty-four checked "Other." Since both these categories contained so few respondents, we have dropped them from consideration. Finally, since only thirty-seven respondents characterized their political orientation as "Strong Conservative," we have combined this category with "Moderate Conservative" for purposes of analysis. Nevertheless, our findings also reveal that, when compared to other mental health professionals, psychiatrists are less liberal than psychoanalysts, clinical psychologists, or psychiatric social workers (see Table 15). Psychiatry has both a smaller proportion of strongly liberal and a larger proportion of conservative practitioners than any of the other three professions. Moreover, this is a true interprofessional difference since the relationship holds when controls are introduced for sex, age, social class origins, and cultural affinity. Thus our findings in Table 15 raise two general questions: why are the members of all the mental health professions predominantly liberal in their political orientation, and what factors peculiar to the various occupational groups may account for the observed interprofessional differences in political perspectives?

Among the many factors that may contribute to the distribution of political orientations in the mental health professions, two are of particular importance. The first is the process of professional socialization undergone by trainees in each of the professions. That is, aspirants in the mental health professions may undergo experiences during the course of professional education and training that tend to push them in the direction of political liberalism. The second factor is selective recruitment. This interpretation rests on the assumption that individuals with a background of particular values and attitudes tend to choose careers in occupations that reinforce those backgrounds more frequently than they choose vocations less congruent with their past; conversely, occupations, through their institutions, tend to choose individuals whose values and attitudes are in harmony with those held by the established occupational membership. Undoubtedly, both processes are involved in determining the political composition of the mental health professions. It is also likely that the two processes do not exercise equal influence in determining the distribution of political orientations among mental health professionals.

Unfortunately, it is not possible, in the present study, to directly compare the relative power of the processes of socialization against that of selective recruitment. However, it is possible to ap-

Table 15. PROFESSION BY POLITICAL ORIENTATION

Respondent's Political Orientation	PROFESSION Psychoanalyst	Psychiatrist	Clinical Psychologist	Psychiatric Social Worker	Total
	Per Cent and (Base Number)				
Strong Liberal	37.1 (231)	22.9 (163)	41.0 (578)	42.9 (482)	37.6 (1454)
Moderate Liberal	55.1 (343)	53.0 (378)	46.7 (658)	50.8 (571)	50.4 (1950)
Conservative	7.7 (48)	24.1 (172)	12.3 (173)	6.3 (71)	12.0 (464)
Total	99.9 (622)	100.0 (713)	100.0 (1409)	100.0 (1124)	100.0 (3868)

No answer = 124

$\chi^2 = 188.80$, $p < .05$

proach this issue indirectly by assessing the extent to which selective recruitment accounts for the distribution of political orientations in the mental health professions. Since the accuracy of this assessment is directly dependent on the way in which political position is measured, the categories of political orientation require some detailed comment. In general, the various self-designated political orientations derived from the questionnaire will be used to examine the relationship between professional affiliation and political background. These categories of political orientation are very broad and do not refer to specific political positions. However, the interview respondents not only checked the questionnaire item dealing with their current political orientation and that of their parents but also discussed both these political dimensions during the course of the interview. Thus, on the basis of the interview sample, it is possible to suggest what types of specific political positions are subsumed under the general labels of political orientation derived from the questionnaire. Specifically, respondents who checked the category Strong Liberal on the questionnaire most often used such terms as Radical, American Socialist, and Left-winger to define their position during the interview. The category Moderate Liberal was used by persons who identified themselves as a Liberal Democrat, Progressive Liberal, or Left-wing Democrat. Finally, persons classified as Conservative include those who designate themselves as Conservative Democrat, Liberal Republican, or Independent.

Measurement of Political Orientation

In terms of the measurement of political orientation, our data provide only a cross-sectional description of current position. Our interest in selective recruitment, however, requires longitudinal data on practitioners' political biographies. That is, we want to compare those mental health professionals who currently adhere to the political perspective in which they were raised with those who have rejected their political background and adopted some alternative position. To classify respondents in terms of their political biographies, it is necessary to ascertain the political positions to which they were exposed during childhood as well as their current political orientation. If we assume that the political position of parents represents the orientation to which the respondent was exposed during childhood, it is possible, by comparing it to the practitioner's current political orientation, to construct an indirect measure of political biography. Comparison of practitioners' current political orientations with those they ascribe to their fathers reveals six types of political biographies: Strong Liberal Adherents, Moderate Liberal Adherents, Conservative Adherents, Strong Liberal Converts, Moderate Liberal Converts, and Conservative Converts.

We found three types of respondent-father congruence, each containing a sizable number of practitioners. Thus, 382 respondents are currently strong liberals and had fathers who were strong liberals. These practitioners are Strong Liberal Adherents. Similarly, 801 practitioners perceived themselves and their fathers to be moderate liberals. These practitioners are the Moderate Liberal Adherents. Finally, 314 respondents claimed that both they and their fathers were politically conservative. The label Conservative Adherents has been applied to these respondents. Taken together, these three political biographies represent 43 per cent of the total sample. Hence adherence to one's political background is a prevalent pattern among mental health professionals. However, the likelihood of remaining true to one's political origins varies by type of orientation. Specifically, the more conservative the professional's political orientation, the greater the likelihood of his holding a position identical to that of his father. That is, 29 per cent of the professionals characterizing themselves as strong liberals had fathers with an identical orientation, but the corresponding figures are 46 per cent for moderate liberals and 77 per cent for conservatives.

Although considerable stability exists in the political biographies of mental health professionals, the findings indicate that the predominant pattern is one of change. There are three major biographies involving change. The first biography consists of the 952 professionals who are currently strong liberals but came from moderate liberal or conservative backgrounds. These practitioners are the Strong Liberal Converts. The second biography, the Moderate Liberal Converts, is composed of the 822 practitioners who came from conservative backgrounds but are currently moderately liberal. The last type consists of Conservative Converts and is represented by the ninety-one practitioners who had liberal backgrounds but are currently politically conservative. In general, then, the vast majority of change has been in the direction of liberalism. In fact, 51 per cent of the professionals in the sample characterize their current political orientation as being more liberal than that of their family. Conversely, among all types of converts, those who have moved in a conservative direction constitute only 5 per cent of the total. Unfortunately, since the number of Conservative Converts is so small, it is not feasible to include this biography in subsequent analyses. One group of respondents who moved in a conservative direction have been excluded from the typology: specifically, 119 respondents who came from strongly liberal backgrounds but who are themselves moderately liberal. The justification for this exclusion rests on two considerations. First, if these practitioners were placed in the Moderate Liberal Convert category this particularly political biography would then consist of a mixture of persons, some who have moved in a liberal direction and others who had moved in a conservative direction. In this situation it would be impossible to compare the Moderate Liberal Converts with other biographies where the shift is all in one direction. The second reason is simply that the number of practitioners moving from a Strong Liberal to a Moderate Liberal position is too small to treat the group as a separate biography.

Results thus far indicate a heavy concentration of politically liberal professionals in the mental health field. To a limited extent this outcome results from recruiting individuals who were raised in liberal families. To a much greater extent, however, the political composition of the professional mental health field reflects the strong tendency for practitioners to be persons who have rejected parental backgrounds in favor of a relatively more liberal political orientation. In short, the liberal composition of the mental health professions reflects conversion rather than lifelong adherence to a liberal political tradition.

Since conversion to liberal views is a prevalent pattern among mental health practitioners in general, it becomes important to determine whether this characteristic applies with equal force to each professional group. Are the various political biographies uniformly distributed among the four mental health professions, or do interprofessional differences exist in the concentration of various biographies? Our findings, contained in Table 16, reveal that the

Table 16. Distribution of Profession by Political Biography[a]

Political Biography	PROFESSION				
	Psychoanalyst	Psychiatrist	Clinical Psychologist	Psychiatric Social Worker	Total
	Per Cent and (Base Number)				
Strong Liberal Adherent	12.9 (70)	8.2 (48)	11.7 (139)	13.1 (125)	11.7 (382)
Moderate Liberal Adherent	28.5 (154)	29.5 (173)	22.0 (262)	22.2 (212)	24.5 (801)
Conservative Adherent	5.7 (31)	19.8 (116)	10.2 (121)	4.8 (46)	9.6 (314)
Strong Liberal Convert	27.0 (146)	18.1 (106)	32.5 (386)	32.8 (314)	29.1 (952)
Moderate Liberal Convert	25.9 (140)	24.4 (143)	23.6 (280)	27.1 (259)	25.1 (822)
Total	100.0 (541)	100.0 (586)	100.0 (1188)	100.0 (956)	100.0 (3271)

No answer = 721

[a] No significant interprofessional differences

distribution of political biographies in psychiatry clearly sets it apart from the other three professions.

We earlier found that psychiatrists were more likely than other practitioners to have a conservative political orientation. Table 16 reveals that psychiatrists are also more likely than other professionals to adhere to the political views of their parents. In fact, the majority of psychiatrists have adopted parental political views as their own. When they do change their political orientation, psychiatrists are more likely to be converted to the position of a moderate rather than a strong liberal. This is in marked contrast to the pattern for psychoanalysts, clinical psychologists, and psychiatric social workers, all of whom are more likely to be strong liberal than moderate liberal converts. Relative to other mental health professionals, then, psychiatrists have both more conservative and more stable political biographies.

Perhaps our most striking general finding in this area is the strong similarity in the distribution of psychoanalysts, clinical psychologists, and psychiatric social workers among the five political biographies. In these three groups, not a single significant interprofessional difference exists among all types of political biography. Since the members of these professions are the products of three markedly different training systems, it does not seem likely that professional socialization is the major mechanism determining the political composition of these practitioners. Rather, on the basis of these data, it seems more plausible to suggest that the political composition of these three professions stems primarily from the recruitment of liberal converts. Similarly, from this perspective the difference between psychiatrists and other professionals can be attributed primarily to differential recruitment rather than to variations in the processes of professional socialization. That is, persons who have not broken with their parental political background are more attracted to psychiatry, whereas those who have made the shift to a more liberal viewpoint are attracted to one of the other three professions. Thus the major influence of the various training systems is primarily one of reinforcing already existing political views rather than of inculcating new orientations.

Finally, although the findings contained in Table 16 enable us to answer several specific questions, they also raise a more general issue. That is, why does the distribution of political biographies within psychiatry differ markedly from that of the other professions? If we accept the proposition that the distribution of political biographies in the four professions represents differential recruitment, the question can be stated more explicitly: what is it about psychoanalysis, clinical psychology, and psychiatric social work that makes these fields attractive to liberal converts, and why is psychiatry more appealing to conservatives and moderate adherents? In attempting to account for this interprofessional difference, we are in the same position as we were formerly with regard to the differential distribution of religious biographies in the four mental health professions. There, it will be recalled, we found psychoanalysts and clinical psychologists much more likely to have rejected parental religious positions and much less likely to currently adhere to any of the three traditional religions than was true for psychiatrists or psychiatric social workers. We thus have a clue to the possible explanation of interprofessional differences in the distribution of political biographies. That is, since both political and religious orientations are concerned with explanations of human behavior, it is quite possible that religious and political biographies are strongly related. Specifically, we would expect practitioners who have changed their political orientation also to have changed their religious orientation. The data required to assess this possibility are presented in Table 17.

Our expectations concerning the "fit" between religious and political biographies are borne out with remarkable consistency. Specifically, political adherence is strongly related to religious adherence in all four professions. In fact, the overwhelming majority of practitioners in each category of political adherence have not changed their religious position. Thus the single largest concentration of both Strong and Moderate Liberal Adherents is found among Jewish Adherents in all professions except psychoanalysis. Among Strong Liberal Adherents only, the second largest concentration of practitioners is found in the Secular Adherent category. The one exception is psychoanalysis, in which Strong Liberal Adherents are equally represented among Jewish and Secular Adherents. Finally, in psychoanalysis, psychiatry, and clinical psychology Conservative Adherents are clustered in the Protestant Adherent category. For psychiatric social work the largest proportion of Con-

Table 17. Profession by Political Biography and Religious Biography

Psychoanalysis (PA), Psychiatry (PT), Clinical Psychology (CP), Psychiatric Social Work (PSW)

Religious Biography	POLITICAL BIOGRAPHY: Strong Liberal Adherent				Moderate Liberal Adherent				Conservative Adherent				Strong Liberal Convert				Moderate Liberal Convert				Total			
	Per Cent																							
	PA	PT	CP	PSW	PA	PT	CP	PSW	PA	PT	CP	PSW	PA	PT	CP	PSW	PA	PT	CP	PSW	PA	PT	CP	PSW
Protestant Adherent	5.8	13.0	3.8	17.8	5.4	12.3	18.0	21.5	44.4	51.0	59.6	31.7	5.9	7.0	11.9	17.6	20.0	22.7	33.8	38.7	11.4	21.0	22.1	24.8
Catholic Adherent	2.9	—	—	2.5	2.0	3.7	9.8	15.4	—	21.0	20.9	51.2	1.5	2.0	1.9	5.6	5.4	7.6	8.8	14.7	2.7	7.2	6.9	11.9
Jewish Adherent	36.2	41.3	38.3	37.3	50.3	59.9	42.6	41.0	25.9	18.0	10.9	7.3	29.4	34.0	30.0	40.1	30.0	34.1	26.5	22.3	36.4	39.2	31.1	33.5
Religious Apostate	18.8	17.4	19.5	15.3	31.5	14.2	20.5	13.8	22.2	9.0	5.5	9.8	43.4	47.0	42.5	27.1	41.5	29.5	24.6	21.0	35.0	23.7	27.0	20.3
Secular Adherent	36.2	28.3	28.3	27.1	10.7	9.9	9.0	8.2	7.4	1.0	3.6	—	19.8	10.0	13.6	9.5	3.1	6.1	6.2	3.3	14.5	8.8	12.8	9.5
Total	(69)	(46)	(133)	(118)	(149)	(162)	(244)	(195)	(27)	(100)	(110)	(41)	(136)	(100)	(360)	(284)	(130)	(132)	(260)	(238)	(511)	(540)	(1107)	(876)

No answer = 127, 194, 47, 278

$\chi^2 = 129.71, 217.41, 406.31, 213.34$

$p < .01$

servative Adherents are Catholics. In sum, those who have not changed their political orientation tend to be practitioners who also have not changed their religious orientation.

The consistency of relationships also holds for those who have changed their political orientation; Strong Liberal Converts are most likely to be Religious Apostates in all professions except psychiatric social work. Similarly, sizable proportions of Moderate Liberal Converts are also Religious Apostates in all the professions, although this pattern is the most prevalent one only for psychoanalysts.

When these findings are summarized, several conclusions emerge that contribute to our understanding of the interprofessional differences in political composition of the four mental health professions. Paramount among these is the unequivocal conclusion that political biographies constitute one dimension of a more general orientation toward the social world. Political orientations summarize, to a certain extent, a wide range of views on the determinants of individual behavior—standards for evaluating behavior as well as prescriptions for desired changes in behavior patterns. Since religious orientations also reflect views on these general issues, understanding of our findings on the differential distribution of political biographies should be increased by viewing them in the context of our earlier findings on religious biographies.

The manner in which political and religious biographies are interrelated is most clearly revealed among the practitioners who have changed their orientations. Specifically, practitioners who have been converted to their current political position tend to be Religious Apostates. We earlier suggested that Religious Apostates are more accepting of the principles of psychological determinism and are concentrated in psychoanalysis and clinical psychology, the two professions that place the greatest reliance on theoretical models and scientific methodology. To understand why political converts also tend to be Religious Apostates, we need only note that the conversions we investigated were all in the direction of increased liberalism. Characteristic of the liberal perspective is the view that behavioral problems can only be eradicated through intervention designed to improve the underlying social and psychological conditions that are the basic causes of undesirable behavior. Hence, for changes to be effectively directed, it is necessary to understand wherein difficulties lie. It follows logically that persons committed to this perspective would be more attracted to the notions of psychological determinism and scientific methodology than to those of indeterminacy, voluntarism, and free will. This would be particularly so, perhaps, for those who have independently adopted their current liberal position rather than inherited it from their family. Thus, taken together, the biographies of Religious Apostates and Strong Liberal Converts reflect a general orientation revolving around a scientific perspective with regard to human behavior.

With regard to political adherents, the relationship between political and religious orientations is clearest for the Conservatives but also applies to Liberal Adherents. Conservatives tend to be either Protestant or Catholic Adherents. Since these two religions place considerably more emphasis on indeterminancy and voluntarism than is true for Judaism, it is understandable that they would be more attractive to politically conservative practitioners. Strong Liberal and Moderate Liberal Adherents also show a strong tendency to have stable religious biographies. However, in keeping with their liberal political views, they are adherents to Judaism, the religion most receptive to scientific explanations of human behavior.

Thus our underlying explanatory model assumes that political stability is related to religious adherence and that the distinction between stable conservative and stable liberal political orientations resides in the willingness of practitioners to accept scientific explanations of human behavior. Hence the relationship between Conservative political adherence and Protestant or Catholic religious adherence is taken to reflect a preference for the principles of indeterminacy and free will. In a similar vein, the relationship between Strong Liberal and Moderate Liberal political adherence and Jewish religious adherence is assumed to reflect a somewhat greater willingness on the part of practitioners to rely on scientific explanations of behavior. Finally, we also assume that changes in political orientations are related to changes in religious orientations and that both reflect conversion to a position of strong commitment to explaining human behavior in terms of scientific principles. The relationship between conversion to a liberal political position and Religious Apostasy is a reflection of this general scientific orientation.

With this explanatory model it is possible to elucidate, at least in part, the interprofessional differences in the distribution of political biographies. Psychiatry has both the largest proportion of members with stable political biographies and the largest proportion of conservative practitioners because it is more attractive to people not strongly committed to scientific determinism and theoretical closure. Conversely, persons receptive to the principles of scientific determinism and accepting of theoretical frameworks and conceptualization are more likely to be political converts and to become psychoanalysts or clinical psychologists. Finally, psychiatric social work represents a deviant case in terms of our explanatory model. That is, psychiatric social workers are fully as likely as psychoanalysts or clinical psychologists to be Strong Liberal Adherents, but they tend also to be Jewish Adherents rather than Religious Apostates. The explanation for this exception may lie in the fact that psychiatric social work is the most overtly political of all mental health professions. That is, psychiatric social work emerged from the social reform tradition of general social work and still has strong ties to welfare and community service organizations. Indeed, psychiatric social workers are frequently employed in action-oriented programs and community organizations. For this reason, psychiatric social work may represent an obvious career line for someone coming from a politically liberal Jewish background. This fact may be particularly true for women. In any case, it seems apparent that psychiatric social work represents a deviant case and does not, by itself, negate the general pattern we have outlined.

Finally, it should be noted that our explanation of the political background of psychiatric social workers implies that the salient factor affecting entrance into the profession is not simply political allegiance but also level of political involvement of parents. Fortunately, it is possible, by using the interview data, to empirically assess this possibility for all four mental health professions. The descriptions of political involvement of parents given in the interviews were grouped into the following three categories: active involvement, which refers to participation in activities and organizations clearly designed to effect political ends; passive involvement, which refers to individuals who manifest interest and affective involvement in political affairs and who may have membership in one or more political organizations but minimal or no active participation; and weak or no involvement, referring to individuals who manifest low interest and involvement in political affairs and for whom voting is the only political activity. Using these dimensions, we find, in the first two sets of figures in Table 18, that less than one-fifth of all fathers were politically active and less than one-tenth of all mothers were active. More importantly, we find significant interprofessional differences, which vary from one parent to another. Regarding fathers' political involvement, twice as many social workers' fathers were politically active as were the fathers of psychoanalysts and clinical psychologists, and they in turn were twice as often classified as active as were the fathers of psychiatrists.

Regarding mothers' political involvement, social workers' mothers again are significantly more active than the mothers of the other three groups of professionals. But here there is no further differentiation among the mothers of psychoanalysts, clinical psychologists, and psychiatrists.

Clearly, a significantly larger proportion of our respondents who became psychiatric social workers experienced a more intense political home environment than did respondents who entered the remaining three mental health professions. Moreover, psychiatrists come from homes with the weakest political climate. Psychoanalysts and psychologists come from political environments roughly midway between those of social workers and psychiatrists, in terms of involvement with political issues.

These differences along the dimension of parental political involvement are genuine professional differences: they hold when controls are introduced for differences in sex, age, ethnic origins, and social class origins. In attempting to understand them, we are in the same situation as we were formerly in attempting to explain why, among potential candidates for the mental health professions, those who were most religious would tend to choose social work. Hence we adopt the same logic and assert, first, that the more politically active the parents, the more politically active their children,

Table 18. INTERPROFESSIONAL COMPARISON: PARENTAL AND RESPONDENT POLITICAL INVOLVEMENT

Fathers' (F), Mothers' (M), Respondents' (R)

Degree of Involvement	Psychoanalyst			Psychiatrist			Clinical Psychologist			Psychiatric Social Worker			Total		
	Per Cent														
	F	M	R	F	M	R	F	M	R	F	M	R	F	M	R
Active	7.8	2.4	4.0	16.3	3.0	17.8	15.1	2.4	14.3	31.8	15.0	17.5	17.3	5.7	13.1
Passive or None	92.2	97.6	96.0	83.7	97.0	82.2	84.9	97.7	85.7	68.2	85.0	82.5	82.7	94.3	86.9
Total	(51)	(42)	(60)	(43)	(33)	(45)	(53)	(42)	(56)	(44)	(40)	(40)	(191)	(157)	(191)

and, second, that the cultural images of the four mental health professions are differentially attractive to those who are politically concerned.

This explanation, of course, requires that the professions be characterized in terms of those dimensions of their political images that have salience for political activity. We have already identified social work as the most overtly political of the four professions. Its interest in social reform and its working relationships with social welfare agencies, with community organizations, and with government institutions such as juvenile courts have contributed to its image as at least the most politically cognizant, if not active, of the professions, especially in contradistinction to the aloof private practice identities of psychoanalysis and psychiatry. Thus it is understandable that those with intense political concerns would gravitate toward social work, which clearly provides an arena for their expression.

It is far less clear why psychoanalysis and clinical psychology differ from psychiatry in their greater appeal to those who value political action. One clue resides in the finding that fathers' political orientation is generally related to fathers' degree of political involvement in such a way that the more politically active the father, the farther left his political orientation is likely to be. Conversely, the more politically conservative he is, the less politically active he is. Psychiatry, then—if our earlier characterization of it as politically conservative (relative to psychoanalysis and clinical psychology) is accurate—would tend to draw candidates from less politically active families.

It was at the level of political orientation that we earlier suggested that a liberal perspective was consistent with the acceptance of the scientific explanation of human behavior. If political involvement reflects political orientation, and if political perspective in turn summarizes a general orientation to the social world, then we might well expect interprofessional differences in the level of current political involvement. The third set of figures in Table 18 presents the data on this dimension.

The sole interprofessional difference on this issue contrasts the fewer politically active psychiatrists with the more frequently active psychoanalysts, psychologists, and social workers. This finding is, of course, in line with the fewer liberally oriented psychiatrists; for, as was the case with fathers, there is a relationship between the professionals' orientation and involvement: the more left one's orientation, the more likely he is to be politically active. In sum, it is political orientation and not political activity per se that is the salient dimension in the background of mental health professionals.

VI

Evolution of Professional Choice

Recruitment into professional careers often begins with the emergence of vocational interests and aptitudes in childhood and is followed by crystallization of these interests as the individual progresses through stages of formal education. Available research on occupational choice has highlighted the importance of "significant others," particularly parents, in choice of a career (Barron, 1969; Super and Bachrach, 1957; Ginzberg et al., 1951). For example, the expectations of significant others have been found to influence a person's conception of his own ability, his cognitive and motivational orientations toward various occupations, and his occupational aspirations and preferences (Sewell, Haller, and Portes, 1969). The family, other key figures, and experiences undoubtedly affect initial or primary vocational choice—for example, medicine, psychology, or social work. However, there has been relatively little research into the later evolution of vocational interests that result in a secondary choice—that is, a specialty within the parent discipline. Hence the extent to which existing generalizations concerning the process of occupational choice can be extended to the selection of a professional specialty is an issue requiring empirical investigation. Our purpose is to conduct such an investigation on the mental health professionals. By focusing on choice of a particular specialty within medicine, psychology, and social work, rather than simply on the choice of one of these general disciplines, we intend not only to explore the relationship between primary and secondary occupational choice but also to provide some baseline data on the evolution of vocational interests in one occupational sphere.

For purposes of our investigation, occupational choice is seen as a long-term developmental process consisting of a series of choice points in a person's life, each of which narrows the range of existing career alternatives until ultimately the choice of a particular career is made (Blau et al., 1956; Super, 1953; Ginzberg et al., 1951). Our objective is to identify the various persons and experiences that contributed, at various stages in the occupational decision-making process, to the final choice of a career in one of the four mental health professions. However, the various stages in the process of selecting a career in one of the professional specialties in the mental health field have not been systematically documented. Consequently, we will begin our examination of occupational choice by identifying the various stages in the process of choosing a career in one of the professional specialties. To achieve this objective, we will use the survey data, thereby maximizing breadth of coverage. We will then turn to a consideration of the evolution of vocational interests and use the interview data to identify the various persons and experiences that influenced the ultimate selection of a career as a psychotherapist.

Stages in the Process of Occupational Choice

Age of Occupational Interest: The four mental health professions possess many related and partially overlapping functions and responsibilities in sharing the general societal mandate to treat mental illness. However, the members of these professions represent the end product of four markedly different training systems. To a certain extent these differences reflect the three major routes into the mental health field—namely, medicine, psychology, and social work. Thus, to understand the process of occupational choice, it is important to determine whether entry into the field follows initial interest in one of the "parent" disciplines or whether it results from an early interest in psychiatry, psychoanalysis, clinical psychology, or psychiatric social work per se. The mean age at which interest in these various areas develops is presented in Table 19.

For psychoanalysts and psychiatrists the earliest interest, which occurs at 14 or 15 years of age, is in medicine. This interest is followed, at age 17 to 19, by an interest in psychology by 22 per cent of the psychoanalysts and an identical percentage of psychiatrists. Interest in psychiatry occurs for both groups of medical professionals at approximately age 23, followed two years later by an interest in psychoanalysis. Psychoanalysts become interested in medicine, psychology, and psychiatry at a somewhat earlier age than do psychiatrists, but this difference disappears by the time these doctors develop an interest in psychoanalysis. In short, the evidence does not support the view that many analysts develop an early interest in psychoanalysis and view their subsequent medical training solely as a means to this end.

Table 19. Mean Age of Interest in Mental Health Professions

	PROFESSION			
	Psycho-analyst	Psychia-trist	Clinical Psychol-ogist	Psychiatric Social Worker
	Per Cent and (Base Number)			
Medicine	14.0 (527)	15.0 (597)	14.9 (273)	14.9 (142)
Psychiatry	22.6 (528)	23.8 (618)	18.2 (147)	— —
Psychoanalysis	25.3 (536)	25.5 (252)	24.8 (412)	24.9 (109)
Psychology	17.0 (117)	19.0 (136)	20.7 (1158)	19.2 (255)
Clinical Psychology			23.4 (1028)	20.8 (131)
Social Work				21.7 (925)
Psychiatric Social Work				25.9 (716)

Psychologists develop an interest in psychology around the age of 21, which is considerably later than the age at which the medically trained professionals develop their initial interest in medicine. However, it should be noted that a considerable proportion of psychologists (24 per cent) were also interested at one point in medicine, and this too was at a much earlier age. In fact, the mean age of interest in medicine for psychologists is about the same as it is for psychiatrists and psychoanalysts. The same is true for those social workers (15 per cent of the total) who at one time had an interest in medicine. Thus the early age of interest among medical professionals reflects the fact that medicine is a profession whose duties are more clearly defined and readily apparent to young people than are those of the psychologist or social worker. In short, it is the differential visibility of the professions rather than individual characteristics of recruits, such as psychological readiness for occupational commitment, that results in temporal variations in occupational interest.

For the psychologist, interest in the professional specialty of clinical psychology develops about two years after the initial interest in general psychology. Interest in clinical psychology is followed, for 36 per cent of the psychologists, by an interest in psychoanalysis. Thus, although those who enter the mental health field through psychology develop an interest in their particular field somewhat later than do those who enter the field through medicine, they develop subsequent professional interests at a somewhat quicker pace; as a result, they end up being interested in psychoanalysis at about the same age as do psychoanalysts.

Social workers are the last to develop an interest in their particular profession. The average social worker was almost 22 years old before he developed his interest in the field. This delay reflects, in part, the fact that many social workers had prior interests in other fields. Specifically, before developing an interest in social work, 15 per cent of all social workers had an interest in medicine, 28 per cent had an interest in psychology, and 14 per cent an interest in clinical psychology. Moreover, these prior interests developed relatively early, particularly in comparison to the age of interest of psychologists in both general and clinical psychology. In sum, although many social workers became interested in general and clinical psychology as undergraduates, they tended not to develop an interest in social work until after college graduation. Finally, it is several years after the initial interest in social work that an interest in *psychiatric* social work is specifically expressed. This delay undoubtedly reflects the fact that many social workers acquire an interest in the psychiatric specialty of their profession only after being employed for some time.

In examining age of interest in the mental health professions, it is important to remember that all four professions are relatively young and rapidly growing occupational groups. Clinical psychology and psychiatric social work both experienced a rapid growth in the number of training programs as well as a broadening of the range of functions performed by practitioners in the mental health field following World War II. As a result, the mental health professions undoubtedly became much more visible to potential recruits after the war than had been true earlier. Thus, to the extent that the visibility of a professional field affects the age at which young people become interested in it as a career possibility, we would expect younger practitioners to have developed an interest in their profession at an earlier age than their older colleagues. Table 20 reveals that this fact is true for age of interest in the parent professions and also holds for age of interest in a specific profession. Thus, when the members of each profession are divided into four age groups—under 40, 40–49, 50–59, and 60 or over—the means for the successive age groups increase consistently, with the earliest interest being shown by the youngest age group. Since sizable numbers of practitioners in each profession expressed an interest at some time in psychoanalysis, we included this specialty as a separate comparison. Here again, we note that the increased visibility and popularity of psychoanalysis have led to a direct relationship between age of interest and age of the professional.

Although the difference in favor of earlier development of interest by young practitioners is consistent across all fields of interest, the amount of this age difference varies considerably. Interest in the medical field by psychiatrists and psychoanalysts shows the least change over time, with the youngest groups developing an interest approximately three years earlier than the oldest age groups. Interest in the respective parent professions by clinical psychologists

Table 20. MEAN AGE OF OCCUPATIONAL INTEREST BY PROFESSION AND AGE OF RESPONDENT

In Field[a] (F), in Specific Profession[b] (SP), in Psychoanalysis (P)

Age of Respondent	PROFESSION											
	Psychoanalyst			Psychiatrist			Clinical Psychologist			Psychiatric Social Worker		
	F	SP	P	F	SP	P	F	SP	P	F	SP	P
Under 40	13.2	19.7	22.3	14.0	20.2	22.7	18.9	20.3	21.2	20.2	22.7	22.6
40–49	14.1	22.1	24.1	14.8	23.3	24.9	20.5	23.1	24.9	21.3	25.6	25.5
50–59	13.5	24.1	28.0	15.4	26.3	29.4	23.3	27.6	29.4	23.6	29.4	27.1
60 and over	16.3	25.6	28.5	16.9	28.5	29.4	23.1	30.7	30.8	24.3	32.5	30.0
Total Number of Respondents	(527)	(628)	(536)	(597)	(618)	(252)	(1158)	(1028)	(412)	(925)	(716)	(109)

[a] Age of interest in field refers to age of interest in medicine for psychoanalysts and psychiatrists, age of interest in psychology for clinical psychologists, and age of interest in social work for psychiatric social workers.

[b] Interest in specific profession refers to age of interest in psychiatry for psychiatrists and psychoanalysts, age of interest in clinical psychology by psychologists, and age of interest in psychiatric social work by social workers.

and psychiatric social workers develops about four years earlier among the younger practitioners.

As might be expected, age of interest in the specific professions has dropped even more than age of interest in the parent profession. Clinical psychologists and psychiatric social workers who are under 40 developed an initial interest in their specific profession fully ten years earlier than did their professional colleagues who are 60 or older. Similarly, younger psychiatrists developed an initial interest eight years sooner than did older psychiatrists, and younger psychoanalysts developed an interest six years earlier than did their older colleagues.

Finally, age of interest in psychoanalysis has dropped markedly in all four professions, with the contrast again being somewhat greater among clinical psychologists and psychiatric social workers than among the two medical groups. In general, the professions that show the greatest difference between younger and older practitioners are the most recently established, namely clinical psychology and psychiatric social work.

The earlier development of interests is undoubtedly a general phenomenon not peculiar to the mental health professions; however, the difference may be greater within these professions because of their recent emergence and the greater likelihood of information about them becoming available to people at an early age. Another contributing factor may be found in the increasing likelihood that young people will have actual contact and direct experience with members of these professions. Undoubtedly many factors contribute to this general trend. Certainly increased specialization and the concomitant lengthening of professional training programs increase the necessity for an early occupational decision. Rising costs of higher education may also contribute to shortening the period of occupational indecision, particularly for persons from lower socioeconomic backgrounds. When financial resources are limited, parents are unable to support children for an extended period of "general" education; moreover, financial assistance in the form of fellowships and stipends is frequently tied directly to specific occupational programs. Consequently, the individual is under considerable pressure to make an early occupational decision. Thus social, structural, and individual factors operate to lower the age of initial interest in a profession.

Age of Occupational Decision: The decision to enter a particular occupational field was usually made three or four years after the initial interest in the field by psychoanalysts, psychiatrists, and clinical psychologists. For psychiatric social workers the decision to enter the field occurred approximately three years after initial interest. The decision to enter a specific profession follows the same general pattern for psychiatrists and social workers. However, for clinical psychologists and psychoanalysts the time between interest and decision to enter a specific profession is about one year less than it was for entry into the field.

The decision to enter medicine is the earliest and is made around the age of 18 by both psychiatrists and psychoanalysts. Psychiatrists decide to enter the profession of psychiatry nine years after making the decision to enter medicine, whereas psychoanalysts take approximately eight years to make the identical decision. However, once they have made the initial decision to enter psychiatry, it only takes analysts about three years to decide on psychoanalysis. That is, the mean age at which practitioners decide to go into psychoanalysis is 29. Since the decision to enter psychiatry and the decision to enter psychoanalysis occur during the late twenties for most medically trained people, it is clear that these decisions are made during training. Few psychiatrists or psychoanalysts make these decisions before completing medical school. In fact, only 10 per cent of the psychiatrists and 13 per cent of the psychoanalysts had made this decision by the age of 20 and only about one-third of each group had decided on psychiatry before the age of 25. Thus, although exposure to psychiatry in medical school may have aroused interest in the profession, it is generally not until trainees complete internships that the decision to become a psychiatrist is finalized.

Social workers and psychologists make the decision to enter their professional fields about the same time; the mean age of decision in both groups is 24. However, social workers make the decision to enter psychiatric social work nearly two years later than psychologists decide on clinical psychology. Undoubtedly this difference reflects the fact, mentioned earlier, that psychiatric social work is a less clearly differentiated professional specialty than clinical psychology and the development of interest in this specialty is more dependent on actual field experience. Additional support for this interpretation is gained by comparing the mean age of interest and decision of psychologists with those of social workers. Specifically, the mean age of interest in clinical psychology occurs *before* the decision to enter the general field of psychology, but the mean age of interest in psychiatric social work occurs *after* the decision to enter the general field of social work. In sum, interest in clinical psychology develops during training and before actual experience in the field, but interest in psychiatric social work is a refinement of interest in social work and arises out of field experience. Thus, although all four groups follow the same general process of occupational choice, in which interests are progressively refined from the general to the specific, considerable variation does exist among the professions with regard to the identifiable choice points.

As with age of interest, age of decision is directly related to age of practitioner. As revealed in Table 21, this relationship holds for both decision to enter the professional field and decision to enter a professional specialty. However, although the earlier choice by younger professionals is true for all fields and specialties involved, the amount of difference between age groups is greatest for the decisions to enter the specialties of psychiatric social work and clinical psychology and least for the decision to enter general medicine. As might be expected, age differences are greater for the decision to enter psychiatry than they are for the decision to enter medicine but less than the differences existing in the age of decision to enter either clinical psychology or psychiatric social work. Specifically, the decision to enter medicine occurs approximately two years earlier among younger psychiatrists and psychoanalysts, compared to the older members of their profession. A similar comparison regarding the decision to enter psychiatry yields a six-year difference for psychoanalysts and an eight-year difference for psychiatrists. The decision in psychology occurs approximately seven years earlier in the youngest group compared to the oldest, but the decision to enter clinical psychology is made twelve years sooner by the youngest group. Finally, there is a six-year differential in age of decision to

Table 21. MEAN AGE OF OCCUPATIONAL DECISION BY PROFESSION AND AGE OF PRACTITIONER

In Field (F), in Specific Profession (SP)

Age of Practitioner	PROFESSION							
	Psychoanalyst		Psychiatrist		Clinical Psychologist		Psychiatric Social Worker	
	F	SP	F	SP	F	SP	F	SP
Under 40	17.6	23.5	17.9	24.1	21.3	22.3	22.5	24.1
40–49	17.7	25.0	18.8	27.3	24.2	25.9	23.6	27.5
50–59	17.7	28.6	18.8	30.2	29.1	31.3	26.5	32.5
60 and over	19.8	29.2	19.8	32.3	28.7	34.2	28.4	33.8
Total Number of Respondents	(493)	(631)	(571)	(639)	(945)	(1079)	(841)	(793)

enter social work and a ten-year differential in the age of decision to enter psychiatric social work.

In general, then, it is in the newer professional specialties where we find the greatest difference between younger and older practitioners with regard to age of occupational decision. Thus one concomitant of the development of extensive training programs in a professional specialty is a drop in the age at which trainees decide to become specialists—at least in the mental health professions. Moreover, not only does the mean age of occupational decision drop, but the variance around this mean also decreases as we move from the oldest to the youngest group of practitioners. Hence institutionalization of a professional specialty in the mental health field results in earlier career decisions and also standardizes the process of occupational decision-making.

Stability of Occupational Choice: Our findings documenting the relationship between the extent to which a professional specialty in the mental health field is institutionalized and age of occupational interest and decision suggest that interprofessional differences may also exist in the stability of occupational choice. Specifically, the findings lead us to expect a larger proportion of both clinical psychologists and psychiatric social workers than psychiatrists or psychoanalysts to have considered other occupations prior to making a final decision. Data on changing occupational plans come from responses given to the following questionnaire item: "Did you seriously consider preparing for an occupation other than your current one at any time after you graduated from high school?"

Other occupations were considered by 83 per cent of clinical psychologists and by 74 per cent of psychiatric social workers but by only 53 per cent of psychoanalysts and 49 per cent of psychiatrists. Thus members of the two medical professions make their occupational decisions earliest and are least likely to consider an alternative after graduating from high school. Since psychologists do not decide on psychology until they are past 20, on the average, they are naturally still considering alternatives for some time following graduation from high school. Although social workers say that their decision was made at an even later date, on the average, than that claimed by psychologists, somewhat fewer admit to considering other occupations after high school. Apparently they consider social work as a career for a period of time before the actual decision and during that period do not actively consider other occupations. In any case, it is clear that the lengthy, standardized training program for psychiatrists and psychoanalysts effectively precludes serious consideration of other occupations following graduation from high school (Rosenberg, 1957).

Since extensive training programs have only recently been developed in clinical psychology and psychiatric social work, we might expect the proportion considering other occupations to be lower among younger members of these professions. However, there is no difference among the four age groups in these two professions. Even more surprising, perhaps, is the finding that younger psychiatrists and psychoanalysts are more likely to have considered another occupation than are older members of these two professions. In short, the impact of age on the stability of occupational choice is confined to precisely those professions that have the most fully developed training programs. The explanation of this finding lies, perhaps, in the increasing number of professional specialties, both in the mental health field and elsewhere. That is, the emergence of new professional specialties may enable the young person to consider various alternative careers before making a relatively early decision to enter psychiatry. Support for this possibility is contained in Table 22, which shows the types of occupations considered by mental health professionals before they made their final decision.

The occupations considered by members of the various professional groups prior to making the final choice tend to be in the general area of the final professional choice. Thus about half the psychiatrists and psychoanalysts seriously considered other occupations in the physical and biological sciences. Among social workers who changed their occupational plans about half seriously considered some other major profession (journalism, law, teaching, ministry, architecture) prior to deciding on their present profession. Psychologists tended to be somewhat higher than the other professional groups in the earlier choice of an occupation in the fields of humanities, arts, and business, although they are most likely to have seriously considered some other major profession before deciding on psychology. Thus the other occupations considered by psychiatrists and psychoanalysts tended to be other professional specialties in the

Table 22. OTHER OCCUPATIONS CONSIDERED BY PROFESSION

	PROFESSION			
	Psychoanalyst	Psychiatrist	Clinical Psychologist	Psychiatric Social Worker
	Per Cent			
Physical Science	23.6	24.1	12.0	5.8
Medicine-Biological Sciences	29.3	26.2	22.6	17.3
Social Science	5.4	5.2	2.5	7.1
Other Mental Health Professions	3.8	3.0	4.7	3.5
Other Professions	21.0	22.9	35.3	47.1
Humanities, Arts, Business, Other	16.9	18.6	22.9	19.2
Total[a]	100.0	100.0	100.0	100.0
	(314)	(328)	(1178)	(848)

No answer = 181

$\chi^2 = 168.29$, $p < .01$

[a] Does not apply = 1143

medical and physical science field. However, very few psychiatrists and psychoanalysts considered other mental health professions. Since few clinical psychologists and psychiatric social workers considered other mental health professions, we are led to conclude that the emergence of professional specialties in the mental health field has not noticeably changed the process of occupational choice. In fact, even when practitioner age is taken into account, there is no indication of an increase in the frequency of considering other mental health professions prior to making a final occupational choice. Instead, it is in the fields of the physical and biological sciences where we find practitioner age related to initial choice of an occupation other than the one finally selected. Specifically, younger practitioners are more likely than older practitioners to have seriously considered a career in the physical and biological sciences in each profession except psychiatric social work. Young psychiatric social workers are less likely than their older colleagues to have initially considered some other major profession and slightly more likely to have considered a career in the humanities and arts, as well as the physical and biological sciences. In sum, the newer professional specialties in the physical and biological sciences constitute the major career alternatives for mental health professionals, particularly psychoanalysts and psychiatrists.

Thus far we have found that the majority of mental health professionals seriously considered another occupation before making their final occupational decision. We have also presented evidence indicating that, in terms of types of occupations considered, professional specialties outside the mental health field constitute the most prevalent alternatives. A major question yet to be answered concerns the reasons why mental health professionals changed their occupational plans. On the basis of responses to a questionnaire item dealing with this issue, we were able to group the factors resulting in a change in occupational plans into the following five categories: *personal factors* (changing opinion of one's abilities, personal problems, differing judgments about interests or likes and dislikes); *situational factors* (financial reasons, military service requirements, inability to secure academic training, inability to implement occupational plans); *interpersonal factors* (influence of some other person); *field contact factors* (job satisfaction or lack of it, influence of work experience); and *educational factors* (content of curriculum, degree requirements, length of training). As revealed in Table 23, personal factors account for the change in choice of

Table 23. FACTORS IN CHANGING OCCUPATIONAL CHOICE BY PROFESSION

	PROFESSION			
	Psycho-analyst	Psychia-trist	Clinical Psychol-ogist	Psychiatric Social Worker
	Per Cent			
Personal	50.5	54.2	44.0	35.3
Situational	14.1	15.8	25.7	31.3
Interpersonal	10.1	10.8	6.3	4.7
Field Contact	14.7	13.7	17.9	22.9
Educational	10.6	5.5	6.0	5.8
Total[a]	100.0	100.0	99.9	100.0
	(348)	(380)	(1217)	(868)

No answer = 36
$\chi^2 = 113.69$, $p < .01$
[a] Does not apply = 1143

occupation for the majority of psychiatrists and psychoanalysts who did in fact change—significantly more than for the proportion of psychologists or social workers who changed for this reason. Conversely, situational factors account for only about 15 per cent of the change in occupational choice of psychoanalysts and psychiatrists—a considerably smaller proportion than of clinical psychologists or psychiatric social workers. Finally, social workers, more frequently than members of any other professional group, changed because of contact with the field.

We can only speculate on the reasons for these differences. We do know that the somewhat higher socioeconomic background of psychoanalysts and psychiatrists would make freedom of choice more possible: situational factors that could be overcome with financial resources would be less likely to stand in their way. For the medically trained professionals the final choice was probably not far removed from the initial choice, inasmuch as the chief alternative occupations considered were in the fields of physical and biological sciences.

As noted earlier, the occupations considered first by clinical psychologists and psychiatric social workers included a variety of other major professions—law, journalism, teaching, and so on. Situational factors that would prevent completion of such occupational plans may be more easily overcome in clinical psychology, with its increase in training facilities during the past three decades and its general availability of training grants. In the case of psychiatric social work, the shortness of the degree program and the certainty of employment may have made it an attractive alternative for those whose other plans were blocked by situational obstacles.

In general, with regard to reasons for changing occupational plans, the major distinction is between professionals who have received medical training and those who have not received such training. For medically trained professionals the reasons for changing their initial occupational choice and entering the mental health professions are primarily internal preferences and motives. For practitioners who did not enter the mental health field through medicine, the major reasons for dropping an earlier choice and choosing a mental health profession result mainly from external forces and conditions. Thus, although "personal factors" is the single most frequently mentioned category in all four professions, the extent to which a career in the mental health field was viewed, at least initially, as a personal "calling" depends on the specific profession under consideration.

Evolution of Occupational Interests: Influential Figures and Experiences

Our findings concerning the stages in the process of occupational choice provide partial support for the proposition that a person's initial perceptions of a particular field are often vague and that specialization allows him to make a secondary choice that can result in an occupational role more closely approximating his personal needs and interests (Back et al., 1958). Thus we found that selection of a professional specialty in the mental health field resulted from the progressive refinement of interest through four choice points: (1) *interest* in the "field" (defined as medicine for psychoanalysts and psychiatrists, psychology for clinical psychologists, and social work for psychiatric social workers); (2) *decision* to enter the field (defined as above); (3) *interest* in the specific profession (defined as psychiatry for psychoanalysts and psychiatrists, clinical psychology for psychologists, and psychiatric social work for social workers); and (4) *decision* to enter the specific profession (defined as above). This movement from the general field to the specific profession implies that, for many practitioners, the initial view of the particular occupational field was indeed vague. No evidence has been presented thus far, however, concerning the possible factors involved in the progressive refinement of occupational interests leading to the secondary choice of a professional specialty. To explore this issue, we will examine, in some detail, responses given by interview respondents to the following questions dealing with the evolution of occupational interests.

1. When and why did you first become *interested* in the field of (psychiatry, psychoanalysis, clinical psychology, or psychiatric social work)?
   a. Were there any particular *people* who stimulated this interest?
   b. Were there any particular *experiences* that stimulated this interest?
2. When and why did you actually *decide* to become a (psychiatrist, psychoanalyst, clinical psychologist, or psychiatric social worker)?
   a. Were there any particular *people* who stimulated this decision?
   b. Were there any particular *experiences* that stimulated this decision?
3. What do you recall were your reasons at the time for wanting to become a (respondent's profession)?
4. What would you say now as you look back about what your motivations were?

These four questions were repeated for each major prior occupational choice point. For example, a psychoanalyst was further questioned regarding his former interests and decisions regarding psychiatry and medicine. The data produced by these questions enable us to examine five dimensions that intersect at each of the career choice points: persons who exerted influence, the nature of those influences, experiences that exerted influence, the nature of those influences, and the motivations of the individual. Of course, a respondent may speak of several persons or experiences exerting several kinds of influence. A sampling of cases indicated that the following conventions would capture the great majority of responses: two persons, each with space for two types of influences; two experiences, each with space for two types of influence; six motivations. As a result of such multiple answers, the tables presented in this section will consist of the distribution of responses rather than respondents.

Examination of these five dimensions was initially conducted for each of the four stages in the process of choosing a career in one of the mental health professional specialties. However, because the findings are virtually identical for choice points 1 and 2 and for points 3 and 4, we shall present, with two exceptions, only those data relevant to interest in the field and interest in the specific profession. The analysis made clear that, for this sample, interest largely constituted decision. And although there was indeed a time-span averaging between two to four years between initial interest and final commitment (regarding both field and specific profession), little that was new entered the scene during these years, either in terms of influential persons or in terms of changing motivations. Essentially the same forces, needs, and desires continued to operate.

Who exerted influence on the individual at the first choice point of interest in the general field? As revealed in Table 24, the answer depends on which specific profession the respondent ultimately selected. Specifically, of all influential persons discussed, 32 per cent of those reported by psychiatrists and 41 per cent of those reported by psychoanalysts are relatives who were medical professionals. These figures contrast sharply with the small percentage of relatives in their respective fields reported by psychologists and social workers. Taken by itself this interprofessional difference is, perhaps, of limited interest. It becomes considerably more interesting, however, when it is placed in the context of the second major difference between physicians and the nonmedically trained professionals: approximately one-third of all influential persons discussed by psychiatrists and psychoanalysts are parents not in the field, whereas

Table 24. PERSONS INFLUENCING RESPONDENT'S INTEREST IN GENERAL FIELD[a]

Person Discussed	Percentage of Persons Discussed				
	PROFESSION				
	Psychiatrist	Psychoanalyst	Clinical Psychologist	Psychiatric Social Worker	Total
	Per Cent				
Professional in the Field (nonrelative)	22.7	14.7	16.7	46.9	26.6
Parent (not in field)[b]	31.8	29.4	14.3	20.4	23.7
Professional in the Field (relative, including parent)	31.8	41.2	7.1	8.2	20.7
Teacher	6.8	2.9	40.5	16.3	17.2
Other	6.8	11.8	21.4	8.2	11.8
Total Persons Discussed	99.9 (44)	100.0 (34)	100.0 (42)	100.0 (49)	100.0 (169)
Total Respondents	59	49	75	77	260

[a] General field means: for psychoanalysts and psychiatrists—medicine; for clinical psychologists—psychology; for psychiatric social workers—social work.

[b] All interprofessional differences in this table held when controlled for sex, age, social class, and ethnic origins except for this category, where social workers between the ages of 40 and 49 mentioned such figures with a frequency of 32 per cent.

the comparable figures for psychologists and social workers are much smaller (14 per cent and 20 per cent, respectively).

These two medical/nonmedical differences suggest a similar effect: the influence that awakened interest in the field (medicine) in psychiatrists and psycohanalysts was exterted early and from persons close at hand. Roughly two-thirds of the persons they discussed were either parents or relatives. On the other hand, less than a third of the persons discussed by psychologists and social workers fall into these categories. The awakening influences on these groups came from more distant figures and were exerted at a comparatively later time. Thus nearly half the influential persons discussed by social workers are identified as persons in the field (nonrelatives). This figure is two to three times greater than those reported by the other professional groups. To a similar extent, psychologists identify their most influential figure as a teacher.

Varying definitions of who was influential in stimulating interest in the field are related not only to the timing of the influence but also, as revealed in Table 25, to the nature of the influence.

Knowing that parents (both professional and nonprofessional) and relatives (professional) were the two outstanding influential figures for psychiatrists and psychoanalysts, it is not surprising to find these two groups relatively high on two influential role categories: persons who set occupational goals for the respondent and persons who served as role models. The medical/nonmedical distinction is clear-cut on the first of these categories. More than a fourth of the influences discussed by psychiatrists and psychoanalysts fall into this category, whereas the comparable figures for psychologists and social workers are considerably less than one-tenth. However, the distinction appears to break down somewhat on the second category. Psychiatrists and psychoanalysts again report the category with the highest frequency, but they are joined here by psychologists, who give only a slightly lower figure. However, these figures are percentages based on number of influences discussed. When percentages of respondents are compared, approximately one-third of all psychiatrists and psycohanalysts cite at least one figure who served as a role model; less than a fourth of psychologists discuss such figures. Thus it follows that the smaller proportion of psychologists discussed disproportionately more role-model figures. This finding is

Table 25. NATURE OF INFLUENCE[a] EXERTED BY PERSONS CONCERNING RESPONDENT'S INTEREST IN GENERAL FIELD[b]

Percentage of Influences Discussed

Nature of Influence	PROFESSION				
	Psychoanalyst	Psychiatrist	Clinical Psychologist	Psychiatric Social Worker	Total
	Per Cent				
Served as a Role Model for Respondent[c]	47.5	34.0	32.8	14.8	31.2
Exposed Respondent to Field	5.0	15.0	14.5	33.3	17.8
Set Goals for Respondent	27.5	32.1	3.6	7.4	16.8
Stimulated Respondent Intellectually	10.0	5.7	32.7	3.7	13.4
Encouraged Respondent's Interest	5.0	5.7	12.7	24.1	12.4
Other	5.0	7.5	3.6	16.7	8.4
Total Influences Discussed	100.0 (40)	100.0 (53)	99.9 (55)	100.0 (54)	100.0 (202)
Total Respondents	49	59	75	77	260

[a] In the context of decision to enter general field (rather than interest in), an additional category of mode of influence appeared: furnished practical advice. The distribution on this variable was as follows: psychoanalyst, 7.5 per cent; psychiatrist, 8.2 per cent ; clinical psychologist, 13.0 per cent; psychiatric social worker, 19.6 per cent; total, 12.6 per cent.

[b] General field means: for psychoanalysts and psychiatrists—medicine; for clinical psychologists—psychology; for psychiatric social workers—social work.

[c] An exception to this distribution is: for female clinical psychologists, the frequency with which this mode of influence was mentioned is 52.6 per cent.

reasonable, since they were largely talking about teachers, of whom there could be many, whereas psychiatrists and psychoanalysts were largely discussing their parents, of whom there could only be two.

The importance of teachers for psychologists is further revealed by the fact that one-third of these mental health professionals identify intellectual stimulation as an influence, whereas the corresponding figure for the other three professions is 10 per cent or less.

Thus far we have found educational and training figures to have been influential in stimulating initial interest in the field among psychologists and social workers but conspicuously absent as an influence among physicians. To a certain extent this difference undoubtedly reflects the fact that psychiatrists and psychoanalysts become interested in the field earlier than do psychologists and social workers. On the average, physicians become interested in the field at 14 or 15 years of age, whereas the corresponding age for the nonmedical professionals is about 21. However, since the physicians are, in general, adolescents when they become interested in the field, it is possible that various experiences, such as independent reading, work, academic courses, or undergoing psychotherapy, would have been influential in stimulating interest in the field, even if educational and training figures were not. Yet even this general expectation is not borne out by the data. Specifically, four out of every ten social workers had at least one work experience that awakened their interest in the general field. When we examine the nature of the influence produced by the experience, members of this profession are disproportionately high on "being introduced to the field." Similarly, one-third of the psychologists report at least one formal training experience and another one-fifth report at least one reading experience that influenced their initial interest in the field. The dominant nature of the influence exerted by the experience is "intellectual stimulation." On the other hand, only a small number of psychoanalysts and psychiatrists admitted having any influential experiences, and no pattern emerged with regard to either type of experience or nature of its influence. In short, a basic difference between professionals entering the mental health field through medicine and those entering through psychology or social work revolves around the role of influential figures in stimulating initial interest in the field. The exact magnitude of this difference is revealed in

Table 26, which shows the overall figures by profession for all persons and experiences which were seen as influential in determining initial interest in the field.

In their discussion of how they originally became interested in their respective fields, psychologists and social workers are similar in identifying, in approximately equal numbers, both persons and experiences (although a slight edge is on the experience side). In extreme contrast, more than three-quarters of the factors cited by

Table 26. TYPE OF INFLUENCE STIMULATING RESPONDENTS' INTEREST IN GENERAL FIELD

Percentage of Influences Discussed

	PROFESSION				
Type of Influence	Psychiatrist	Psychoanalyst	Clinical Psychologist	Psychiatric Social Worker	Total
			Per Cent		
Persons	78	83	43	48	63
Experiences	22	17	57	52	37
Total	100 (56)	100 (41)	100 (97)	100 (103)	100 (297)

psychiatrists and psychoanalysts are persons. In terms of initial career interest this finding is of central importance, for it integrates all the discrete interprofessional differences existing in timing, sources, and types of influences. Comparatively speaking, both psychiatrists and psychoanalysts, but especially analysts, were directed toward the general field of medicine primarily through "familial dynamics"—either by way of identification with a relative (most frequently a parent) who was a doctor, or through the setting of the goal of becoming a doctor by a parent (who was not in medicine). In short, the influences on psychiatrists and psychoanalysts operated early, consisted of persons rather than experiences, and were expressed through close relationships.

In contradistinction, clinical psychologists and psychiatric social workers were directed to their general fields at a later time and essentially equally by persons and experiences. For psychologists the most important person was the teacher, the most important experiences were training and reading, and the most important mode of influence was intellectual stimulation. For social workers the key figure was the nonrelated professional social worker, the crucial experience was the job, and the chief modes of influence were exposure to the field and the opportunity to recognize their ability and pleasure with the work.

In terms of both timing and range of influences, it is clear that the individual "life-space" involved in commitment to medicine is much more restricted than that involved in commitment to either psychology or social work. Given this distinction, it follows logically that consistent differences should also exist at the level of individual motivations for identifying with a particular professional field. Table 27 reveals that this is indeed the case. In terms of motivations leading to interest in a particular field, social workers are differentiated from the other three professions on three dimensions. Not unexpectedly, the first of these is the desire to help people. Social workers are also distinguished from members of the other professions by the higher frequency with which they reported the need to achieve affiliation with others. Finally, social workers more frequently voiced the desire to help and understand society—that is, to benefit individuals through social change.

The most important motivational category for clinical psychologists, and the one on which their higher frequency separates them from the other professions, is the desire to understand people.

The remaining interprofessional differences shown in Table 27 are based on the medical/nonmedical pairing of the four professions. The most important of these concerns the motive to gain an identity. This motive is most frequently cited by both psychiatrists and psychoanalysts; it is one of those most minimally reported by psychologists and social workers. In a contrary direction, another motive—to understand oneself—also distinguishes analysts and psychiatrists from psychologists and social workers.

Of these six interprofessional differences, five appear to be manifestly congruous with what we have already learned about the different professional patterns of initial field interest. The psycholo-

Table 27. Individual Motivations for Becomnig Interested in General Field

By Percentage of Motivations Discussed

Motivation	PROFESSION				
	Psychoanalyst	Psychiatrist	Clinical Psychologist	Psychiatric Social Worker	Total
			Per Cent		
To Help People	17.9	8.4	12.5	22.7	15.8
To Understand People	6.3	5.9	28.9	12.0	14.4
To Gain Professional Status	12.6	12.6	7.9	7.2	9.6
To Achieve Affiliation with Others	4.2	5.9	5.9	13.7	8.1
To Meet Practical Pressures	9.5	12.6	2.6	9.0	8.1
To Gain an Identity	20.0	13.4	3.3	0.6	7.7
To Understand and Help Oneself	2.1	3.4	10.5	7.2	6.4
To Help and Understand Society	6.3	2.5	3.9	9.0	5.6
Other[a]	21.1	35.3	24.4	18.6	24.4
Total	100.0 (95)	100.0 (119)	99.9 (152)	100.0 (167)	100.1 (533)

[a] Other includes twenty-five different categories of response.

gist's desire to understand others and himself corresponds appropriately to the teacher as his most influential figure, to training and reading as his most influential experiences, and to intellectual stimulation as his most characteristic mode of being influenced.

Similarly, the modal motive of psychiatrists and psychoanalysts—to gain an identity—appears especially appropriate to the professional parent or other relative as their most influential figure, to serving as a role model as the most characteristic mode of being influenced, and to the lack of experience as a factor in generating interest.

Two of the distinguishing motives of social workers—to help people and to help and understand society—also appear fitting to their most influential figure, the professional social worker (who surely would hold and communicate these values), and their most influential experience, the job.

However, it is less clear why social workers should be differentiated by their more frequent reporting of the motive to achieve affiliation with others. Perhaps to some small extent this desire for intense relationships in a work context can be seen as resulting from job experiences that revealed the establishment of such relationships to be instrumental to effective job performance. But the existing data do not clearly make this connection between affiliative relations and helping and understanding; personal involvement with others is seen as a pleasurable end in and of itself. Thus the need for affiliation, compared to other motives leading to an interest in social work, seems to be more independent of influential figures or influential experiences. Furthermore, it appears that social work is seen as a profession in which such needs not only can be satisfied but are appropriate. To a certain extent this attitude may stem from the public stereotype of social work. That is, the popular image of casework involves the empathy and sympathy that characterize the relationship of close friends as opposed to the maintenance of distance and hierarchical distinction that characterize, at least in the lay mind, the process of psychotherapy.

Although there are systematic differences among the professions with regard to the factors stimulating initial interest and commitment to the field, in each case professional choice was based on broad social and personal goals. To a large extent, then, initial occupational choice was based on what Hughes (1955) calls lay conceptions of the occupation. Once choice of a profession is made, the person undergoes socialization designed to transform the lay conceptions about the occupation into the technical orientations of the insider. As a rule this process results in the person's not only acquiring the technical skills of the profession but also internalizing the values of the profession and developing an identification with the professional role. However, for mental health professionals the process does not stop there; either during or after the completion of professional socialization these persons make a secondary choice of a specialty within their professional field. Hence the choice of a specialty is based on the technical orientations of the professional insider. As a result, we would expect the locus of significant figures and experiences to shift from those outside the field to those inside the profession as we move from choice of a professional field to choice of a professional specialty. Table 28 indicates that, with the passing of years and with the change from interest in the general field to interest in the specific profession, there has indeed been a major change in the categories of influential persons: the parent who was not himself a professional is no longer mentioned; his place is taken by the peer.

In terms of interprofessional differences some shifts have also occurred, although there is also a good deal of stability. For example, social workers continue to be differentiated from the other three professions in citing the professional in the field as the most influential figure. This category also becomes salient at this point for psychoanalysts and psychiatrists; more than one-fourth of all persons cited by both groups are so identified.

The identity of the most influential person remains constant for psychologists. The teacher was most frequently discussed in terms of provoking interest in the general field and is still most frequently mentioned as stimulating interest in the specific profession. At the same time, however, the teacher has become a major influence for psychiatrists; about a fourth of the figures they discuss fall into this category.

Although now less salient, the relative who is a professional in the field still captures about a fourth of all mentions by psychiatrists and psychonalysts, and this choice continues to differentiate them on this category from psychologists and social workers.

Table 28. PERSONS INFLUENCING INTEREST IN PROFESSION[a]

By Percentage of Persons Discussed

Person	PROFESSION				
	Psychoanalyst	Psychiatrist	Clinical Psychologist	Psychiatric Social Worker	Total
			Per Cent		
Professional in the Field (nonrelative)	15.6	28.9	25.9	58.8	28.9
Teacher[b]	15.6	26.3	37.0	17.6	24.6
Professional in the Field (relative)	25.0	23.7	7.4	5.9	17.5
Peer[b]	28.1	7.9	18.5	—	14.9
Other	15.6	13.2	11.1	17.6	14.0
Total	99.9	100.0	99.9	99.9	99.9
Total Respondents	(32)	(38)	(27)	(17)	(114)

[a] Profession means: for psychoanalysts and psychiatrists—psychiatry; for psychologists—clinical psychology; for social workers—psychiatric social work.

[b] In the context of decision to enter profession (rather than interest in), the figures for analysts and psychologists change to the effect that teachers become more influential and peers less so.

Given the difference between initial choice of a professional field and the secondary choice of a professional specialty, the shifts noted above are, in general, in the expected direction. That is, after some years of training in the general field, one would expect the importance of the teacher figure to increase. Similarly, since the choice of a professional specialty requires some evaluation of the parent profession, it is understandable that the practicing professional has become a more salient figure for all four groups. Finally, the absence of the parent (not himself a doctor) pushing for medicine is the result of the person's having achieved that end—that is, for these parents the medical *specialty* is unimportant.

However, the prominence of the new influential figure—the peer—was not anticipated. Existing studies of the professionalization process in various occupations indicate that, during professional training, interests shift from broad personal and social goals to an emphasis on professional skills, with the influence of teachers and supervisors increasing (Simpson, 1967; Becker and Geer, 1958; Fox, 1957). Peers apparently do play some role in the process of developing an identification with an occupation (Becker and Carper, 1956). However, the primary interest of trainees, particularly in the advanced stages of training, is in the development of competence in the performance of professional skills, and for this objective peers are seen to have little influence. Hence, since choice of a professional specialty occurs after several years of formal training, we would not expect peers to strongly influence the decision. Among mental health professions this pattern seems to hold for psychiatrists and social workers: only 8 per cent of the influential persons discussed by psychiatrists were peers, and social workers failed to mention even one such figure. However, the pattern clearly does not hold for the other two professional groups: more than one-fourth of all influential persons discussed by respondents who became psychoanalysts (who were becoming interested at this point only in psychiatry) were peers, and nearly one out of every five influential figures mentioned by psychologists were fellow students. These sizable differences clearly cannot be accounted for solely on the basis of differences in the training programs of the various professions, since psychoanalysts and psychiatrists have both undergone medical training. Undoubtedly a wide range of factors would account for the varying influence of peers in the choice of a specialty in the mental health professions. However, one possible explanation lies in the degree of fit between the formal training system and the dominant ethos of each of the professional specialties.

The dominant ethos of both psychoanalysis and clinical psychology revolves around the belief that the ability to modify behavior is primarily dependent on the ability to explain it in terms of cause-and-effect relationships. This ability is achieved by the former through the constantly evolving body of psychoanalytic theory and by the latter through the constant application of the scientific method. These professional ideologies contrast sharply with those of psychiatry and social work. For the latter two groups systems of causation are not of such overwhelming importance; they are not so inextricably linked to what is done. Both professions are more pragmatically oriented, concerned more with how than with why. Psychiatry focuses on treatment per se—on the alleviation of the symptom. Social work focuses on caring for the socially wounded and on creating social reform. The intellectual goals of understanding per se and of contribution to knowledge are less salient for both psychiatry and social work.

Given these differences in ideology, it is clear that the ethos of both psychiatry and social work is more intimately related to the technical content of the training programs that the individuals are involved in at the time when interest in a specialty develops than is the case for either psychoanalysis or clinical psychology. That is, the pragmatic concern with treatment and symptom alleviation in psychiatry fits well with the technical content of the formal medical training program. Similarly, the helping and social reform emphasis of social work lies at the very core of professional education in the field. Since choice of psychiatry or psychiatric social work simply represents extension of the dominant concerns of the parent profession into a specialty field, it is understandable that interest in either of these professional specialties would be aroused primarily by teachers and practicing professionals.

The situation for psychoanalysts is quite different. Psychoanalysis, as a specialty field, is defined more in terms of a body of theoretical knowledge than in terms of technical skills. However, the training of physicians up to the time they develop an interest in a specialty places much more emphasis on technique than on theory. Hence, if physicians who eventually become psychoanalysts are attracted to the specialty because of its theoretical nature, then fellow students who share an intellectual interest in psychoanalytic theory may influence the choice of a professional specialty. Since psychoanalysts are, at the stage of development under examination, developing an interest in psychiatry, this explanation of peer influence rests on the assumption that psychiatrists who go on to become psychoanalysts possess a stronger interest in psychological theory, particularly Freudian theory, at the time they become interested in the specialty of psychiatry than is true for psychiatrists who do not later undertake analytic training. Unfortunately, the amount of available evidence bearing on this issue is sparse. However, the data that do exist tend to support our interpretation. Specifically, the finding that psychoanalysts, on the average, become *interested* in the specialty of psychoanalysis about one year before they *decide* to enter psychiatry strongly suggests that analysts have strong theoretical inclinations that play an important role in their choice of a specialty.

Finally, the situation of clinical psychology falls somewhere in between psychiatry and social work on the one hand and psychoanalysis on the other. The objective of increasing knowledge and understanding of human behavior through the systematic application of the scientific method is, of course, a theme that runs throughout the graduate training program of psychologists. Nevertheless, a clear distinction exists in many graduate departments between clinical psychology and experimental and social psychology. Since the early stages of training in psychology departments are focused primarily on the processes involved in understanding behavior rather than on the processes involved in modifying it, and since the early core courses in the curriculum are rarely taught by clinically oriented faculty, the amount of exposure to and support for a clinical career is somewhat restricted until relatively late in the educational process. Hence it is understandable that psychologists frequently claim that their interest in a clinical career was stimulated informally by peers.

Correspondent with shifts in influential figures between the time of interest in the general field and interest in the professional specialty are changes in the types of influence exerted by significant persons. Specifically, as revealed in Table 29, intellectual stimulation has now replaced role model as the most salient mode of influence: more than one-third of all influences discussed by psychoanalysts, and more than one-fourth of the influences cited by psychiatrists and psychologists, are so categorized. It is only for social workers that intellectual stimulation remains an irrelevant mode of influence.

Nevertheless the category of role model, although of lesser importance at this career point, continues to be reported by about a quarter of the total sample. As before, it is not a powerful mode of influence for social workers. The great change occurring between time of general field interest and time of professional specialty interest on this dimension is for psychoanalysts: during the former period nearly one-half of all personal influences exerted their force by serving as a role model; here the figure is slightly less than one-fifth. Psychiatrists, on the other hand, report virtually identical figures for both career points. This finding represents another indication that psychiatrists view the specialty field much more in terms of technical skills than do psychoanalysts. As a result, psychiatrists are much more likely to adopt their teachers and supervisors as role models. Thus, at this career point, role models are more readily available to physicians interested in the application of treatment techniques to a particular specialty (psychiatrists) than to physicians interested in theoretical models (psychoanalysts).

Also in line with this distinction is the increase in the frequency with which psychoanalysts cite "encouraged interest" as a mode of influence. From a figure of only 5 per cent at time of general field interest, this mode of influence has increased to nearly 20 per cent. Juxtaposing these various changes for psychoanalysts in terms of types of persons and types of influence, we find that the influence of parents (both physicians and nonphysicians) has waned, whereas that of teachers and peers has increased; moreover, the influential modes of serving as a role model and setting goals have declined, whereas those of intellectual stimulation and encouragement have grown. In short, the contrast between choice of a professional field and choice of a professional specialty for psychoanalysts revolves around the refinement of the individual's intellectual interests.

In contrast, psychiatrists have remained relatively more

Table 29. NATURE OF INFLUENCE EXERTED BY SIGNIFICANT PERSONS

By Percentage of Influences Discussed

Nature of Influence	PROFESSION				
	Psychoanalyst	Psychiatrist	Clinical Psychologist	Psychiatric Social Worker	Total
			Per Cent		
Stimulated Respondent Intellectually	35.1	27.1	25.7	5.6	26.1
Served as Role Model for Respondent	18.9	31.2	28.6	5.6	23.9
Exposed Field to Respondent	5.4	18.7	20.0	27.8	16.7
Encouraged Respondent's Interest	18.9	6.2	11.4	44.4	15.9
Gave Practical Advice to Respondent	8.1	12.5	11.4	16.7	11.6
Other	13.5	4.2	2.9	—	5.8
Total	99.9	99.9	100.0	100.1	100.0
Total Respondents	(37)	(48)	(35)	(18)	(138)

stable between time of field interest and time of specialty interest, despite the fact that the influence of parents has waned and that of teachers has increased. But the influence of the professional in the field (nonrelative) has maintained its importance for psychiatrists, and the peer figure makes only an infrequent appearance. Accordingly, the role-model mode of influence remains highly salient for psychiatrists, whereas "encouragement" as a means of influence remains minor. Thus choice of a professional specialty among psychiatrists represents a rather direct refinement of the interests that led them initially into the professional field.

The picture for social workers over time shows no reverses in either figures or modes of influence. On the contrary, those categories that differentiated them from the other professional groups at time of interest in the field continue to do so in a more marked way at time of interest in the professional specialty: the frequency of mention of professional in the field (nonrelative) as influential increased from 47 per cent to 59 per cent, and the "encouraged interest" mode of influence increased from 24 per cent to 44 per cent. Thus for social workers there is no indication that choice of a professional specialty involved reconsideration or refinement of initial occupational interest.

The pattern for psychologists between time of interest in the field and interest in the professional specialty is also a relatively stable one: the teacher remains the most salient influencer, and providing intellectual stimulation and serving as a role model continue to be the principal modes by which this influence was exerted. As for analysts, however, the peer enters the picture as a significant figure regarding interest in professional specialization. Here choice of a professional specialty involves reconsideration of the general field, not so much in terms of rejecting the dominant skill system of the parent profession but in terms of the ways in which those skills are utilized.

Results thus far suggest that both the identity of influential figures and the ways in which they influence interest in a professional specialty are determined, in part, by the extent to which the specialty incorporates elements of the skill system of the parent profession. Another, perhaps more direct, way to assess the influence of parent professions on specialization is to examine the impact of experiences, rather than particular persons, on the choice of a professional specialty. Clearly, if choice of a professional specialty is based on the desire of the individual to modify his occupational role, then experiences that affect the person's image of the profession should play a salient role in stimulating interest in a specialty.

The extent to which choice of a professional specialty results from self-initiated change, rather than from response to particular significant others, is revealed in the changing importance of influential experiences compared to persons from time of interest in the general field to interest in the specialty. Specifically, at time of interest in the general field we saw that the two medical groups differed radically from psychologists and social workers in the greater weight given to persons; the ratio was about 3 to 1 for psychiatrists and 4 to 1 for psychoanalysts. Both psychologists and social workers saw persons and experiences as having roughly equal impact on them (with a slight edge given to experiences). However, at the point of interest in a professional specialty there are essentially no differences between any of the professions. In each case approximately 60 per cent of all influences stem from experiences and 40 per cent from persons. Thus the similarity has been reached in an entirely one-sided manner—that is, it is the medical professionals who have changed. Experiences are now as important for psychoanalysts and psychiatrists as they were and continue to be for psychologists and social workers, and the significance of persons has decreased accordingly.

Although uniformity exists in the relative importance of experiences in precipitating interest in a professional specialty, certain differences are found among the groups in the types of influential experiences (see Table 30). For psychiatric social workers the most important experience in stimulating interest in their professional specialty is the job; four out of every ten experiences reported are of this nature. This finding is consistent with the significance given to this category at the time of interest in the field, when the figure was 57 per cent. The seeming decline is more than made up by the appearance of a new but similar category, field work, which is reported with a frequency of 24 per cent. Taken together as work experiences, these two categories account for almost two-thirds of

Table 30. EXPERIENCES INFLUENCING INTEREST IN THE PROFESSION[a]

By Percentage of Experiences Discussed

Type of Experience	PROFESSION				
	Psychoanalyst	Psychiatrist	Clinical Psychologist	Psychiatric Social Worker	Total
			Per Cent		
Job[b]	35.4	18.0	34.8	41.4	31.2
Training	18.7	36.0	39.1	17.2	28.9
Reading	33.3	22.0	13.0	13.8	21.4
Field Work	12.5	20.0	6.5	24.1	15.0
Other	—	4.0	6.5	3.4	3.5
Total	99.9 (48)	100.0 (50)	99.9 (46)	99.9 (29)	100.0 (173)
Total Respondents	55	63	61	36	217

[a] Profession means: for psychoanalysts and psychiatrists—psychiatry; for psychologists—clinical psychology; for social workers—psychiatric social work.

[b] An exception to this distribution is: the significant order of the four professions on this category—social workers high, analysts and psychologists middle, and psychiatrists low—is true only for males; there is no interprofessional difference here for females.

all experiences discussed and clearly differentiate social workers from the other three groups of professionals.

The nature of influential experiences for psychiatrists has also remained fairly stable. If the current figures for job and field work are combined (38 per cent), the figure is essentially the same as the one-third figure attached to the job at time of interest in medicine. Training, too, remains high and is virtually unchanged from time of interest in field to time of interest in specific profession. What has changed for psychiatrists is the influence of reading; this factor had only negligible effect in determining interest in medicine but constitutes more than one-fifth of all influences that generated interest in psychiatry.

A comparison of clinical psychologists from time of interest in the general field to time of interest in the specific profession reveals a slight deemphasis on the academic (training and reading) influence and an increase in the impact of work experiences (job and field work) in generating interest in clinical psychology.

Psychoanalysts move further in this direction: almost half of all experiences determining their interest in psychiatry are related to work (job and field supervision), whereas formal training accounts for less than one-fifth. Reading, however, accounts for a third of all reported influences, and the magnitude of this figure distinguishes them not only from psychiatrists and social workers but from psychologists as well.

Knowing *what* experiences influenced interest in a professional specialty, it is now possible to ask *how* these experiences stimulated that interest. Table 31 presents the modes of influence exerted by the various experiences. Social workers are differentiated from the other three groups of professionals by the low frequency with which they report intellectual stimulation and the high frequency with which they cite being allowed to recognize potential ability and pleasure in the specific profession. These findings are consistent, respectively, with their infrequent mention of training and reading experiences and their frequent reporting of job and field work experience as most influential. Furthermore, this picture of the impact of experience in determining interest in *psychiatric* social work is virtually identical to that concerning their prior interest in the general field of social work.

Table 31. INTERPROFESSIONAL COMPARISON: NATURE OF INFLUENCE EXERTED BY EXPERIENCE STIMULATING RESPONDENT'S INTEREST IN THE PROFESSION

By Percentage of Influences Discussed

Nature of Influence	PROFESSION				
	Psychoanalyst	Psychiatrist	Clinical Psychologist	Psychiatric Social Worker	Total
			Per Cent		
Stimulated Respondent Intellectually	38.6	45.0	33.9	20.0	36.0
Allowed Respondent to Recognize His Potential for Ability and Pleasure in Profession	31.6	20.0	32.2	51.4	31.8
Introduced Field to Respondent	22.8	23.3	16.9	17.1	20.4
Other	7.0	11.7	16.9	11.4	11.8
Total	100.0	100.0	99.9	99.9	100.0
	(57)	(60)	(59)	(35)	(211)
Total Respondents	55	63	61	37	216

Although intellectual stimulation is the most salient mode of influence for the other three professions, psychiatrists are differentiated by their higher frequency of mention of this category. This finding is consistent with their selection of training and reading as the two most influential experiences. Across the two career points of interest in medicine and interest in psychiatry, these findings suggest only minor change in terms of the frequency with which any given category is mentioned. However, as has been noted, the number of influential experiences reported by psychiatrists concerning interest in psychiatry is more than four times as many as discussed concerning interest in medicine.

Two-thirds of the modes of influence reported by psychologists fall equally into two categories: intellectual stimulation and opportunity for the individual to recognize his ability and pleasure in the profession. These findings follow reasonably well from the equal frequency with which training and job experience are cited as influential experiences. However, these findings concerning interest in *clinical* psychology represent a considerable change from the influential modes associated with earlier interest in the general field. At that time slightly more than half of all influences discussed operated through intellectual stimulation; here the figure has dropped to approximately one-third. This finding follows from the former greater importance attributed to schooling and the current greater emphasis on work experience.

Psychoanalysts present a picture similar to that of psychologists: approximately two-thirds of the modes of influence they report fall more or less equally into the categories of intellectual stimulation and opportunity to recognize ability and pleasure in psychiatric work. And, as with psychologists, this finding represents, over the time period between interest in medicine and interest in psychiatry, a decrease in the emphasis placed on intellectual stimulation and a relative increase in the importance attributed to the opportunity for recognizing one's ability and pleasure in the profession.

When these findings on choice of a specialty are summarized, it is clear that the amount of professional control, either in the form of role models or guidance supervisors, exercised over the choice of a specialty is extremely limited. It is true, of course, that the profession does partially control the range of experience to which the individual may be exposed. It is also clear, however, that in choosing a professional specialty in the mental health field, it is the individual's reaction to selected experiences that is of prime importance. Hence, to gain some understanding of the way in which various experiences are linked to the consequent selection of a particular specialty, it is instructive to ask what the individual's motives were for specializing in psychiatry, clinical psychology, or psychiatric social work. The available data relevant to this question are presented in Table 32.

On our first category of motivation, to understand people, the four groups rank themselves as follows: psychoanalysts, psychologists, psychiatrists, and social workers. When the actual figures in this category are compared with the list of motivations determining interest in the general field, it is clear that striking increases in intellectual curiosity as a motive for professional interests have occurred for the two medical professions, particularly for psychoanalysts. On the other hand, the motive's importance for psychologists and unimportance for social workers have remained fairly constant over time.

For three professional groups—psychoanalysts, psychologists, and social workers—somewhat less than one-fifth of all reported motivations focused on the desire to help people. Psychiatrists are differentiated on this dimension by their lower frequency of mention. In general these figures represent little change from those reported earlier concerning motivations surrounding interest in the general fields.

Although there are no interprofessional differences on the motive "to understand oneself" in Table 32, a comparison of those figures with the percentages on the same dimension at time of interest in general field shows that both medical groups have evidenced a meaningful increase in the desire for self-understanding as a professional motivation.

The need for professional status has undergone some slight shifts: it is now of lesser importance for psychiatrists and psychoanalysts (they now have the M.D. degree), of somewhat greater importance for psychologists (they do not yet have the Ph.D. degree), and of the same minor importance for social workers.

Perhaps the most striking aspect of the data contained in Table 32 is the fact that all four of the explicit categories of motives

Table 32. INDIVIDUAL MOTIVATIONS FOR BECOMING INTERESTED IN PROFESSION

By Percentage of Motivations Discussed

Motivation	PROFESSION				
	Psychoanalyst	Psychiatrist	Clinical Psychologist	Psychiatric Social Worker	Total
			Per Cent		
To Understand People	31.1	18.0	23.8	11.7	21.7
To Help People	17.0	10.5	16.2	18.4	15.1
To Understand and Help Oneself	10.4	11.0	7.0	9.7	9.4
To Gain Professional Status	3.7	8.1	11.4	6.8	7.9
Other[a]	37.8	52.3	41.6	53.4	45.9
Total	100.0	99.9	100.0	100.0	100.0
	(135)	(172)	(185)	(103)	(595)

[a] Included are thirty categories, none of which is mentioned with a frequency of as much as 5 per cent.

account for only slightly more than half of all the motives that were discussed by the sample as a whole. Thus, motives associated with interest in professional specialties, for all four groups of mental health professionals, are, to an important degree, an idiosyncratic matter. It follows that the decision to specialize is largely self-initiated and based on highly individualistic reactions to influential figures and experiences. This situation seems particularly true for psychiatrists and social workers, who differentiate themselves from psychoanalysts and psychologists by the greater heterogeneity of their motives at this career point.

For psychiatrists, clinical psychologists, and psychiatric social workers, the process of occupational choice terminates with entry into the respective specialty field. Hence, by summarizing the findings presented thus far on the evolution of occupational interests in the mental health professions, it is possible to make a limited assessment of the extent to which generalizations concerning the process of initial occupational choice can be extended to the selection of a professional specialty.

Perhaps one of the best documented generalizations in the literature is that individuals choosing different occupations tend to stress different values. Usually these values are not occupationally specific but are of such a generalized nature that they could be satisfied in a variety of different occupations (Rosenberg, 1957; Simpson, 1967; Underhill, 1966; Meyer, 1959). Even though they are all in the same general occupational field, the mental health professions constitute no exception to this generalization.

The secondary choice of a specialty is made after the person has acquired professional skills, knowledge, behavior patterns, and self-identification with the professional role. Thus, although initial choice of medicine, psychology, or social work is based on general conceptions of the professions, choice of a specialty in these fields is made only after considerable knowledge and understanding of the profession have been accumulated. It follows that choice of a professional specialty should be directly constrained by prior occupational socialization. This situation is true for psychiatrists but is clearly not the case for psychoanalysts and social workers and only partially true for psychologists.

Professional training systems are formally designed to produce graduates who have detailed knowledge in a specific area, competence in a limited sphere of technical matters, and self-conceptions and orientations deemed appropriate for a particular profession. The primary responsibility for both the transmission of professional knowledge and skills and the inculcation of appropriate norms and values is seen to reside with the professional faculty. In such a system it is not surprising that students have been found to develop, over time, a heightened concern with professional skills and technical learning. Similarly, when choice of a professional specialty is placed in the context of such a training system, the potential influences are readily discernible. Specifically, if the formal model of professional training does, in fact, capture the salient dimensions of the actual training program of a particular profession, then we would expect choice of a specialty in that profession to be based on occupationally specific values and significant experiences to revolve around training activities. We would also expect to find members of the profession serving as role models. This profile, of course, summarizes our findings concerning the choice of a specialty by psychiatrists. In terms of their reliance on teachers, role models, and training and work experiences, the description also fits the choice of a professional specialty by psychologists. However, clinical psychologists deviate from the model in that they are also influenced to a considerable extent by peers, and they reveal no tendency to supplant the original values that led them into the field—those revolving around an intellectual curiosity about people—with more technical concerns. Social workers move even further in this direction: choice of psychiatric social work as a specialty is apparently affected very little by the professional training system. Thus social workers were influenced by practicing professionals who exposed them to the field and encouraged their interest. Similarly, the significant experiences for social workers were those occurring on the job; little influence was exerted by teachers and little reliance was placed on role models. Finally, the general values that led social workers into the general field—expressed as desire to help people—were never modified and, in fact, operated as the major reason for their deciding to enter the specialty of psychiatric social work.

To a certain extent, the differences existing between psychiatrists, on the one hand, and clinical psychologists and psychiatric social workers, on the other hand, can be attributed to structural variations in the training programs of the three occupational groups. Support for this interpretation comes from findings reported by Becker and Carper (1956): the lack of a clearly defined body of professional knowledge and of work-related social relationships facilitates the maintenance of a general lay conception of an occupation throughout the socialization process, whereas training organized around a clearly delineated body of knowledge and set of task-related relationships leads to the rejection of the layman's conception and the substitution of a technical orientation toward the profession. Since the training of psychiatrists is, in this sense, clearly more highly structured than that of either psychologists or social workers, this interpretation could account for the fact that the values of psychiatrists underwent a transformation in the technical direction but those of the other two groups of professionals did not. Structural variation in training programs may also account for the fact that psychologists were more influenced in their choice of a specialty by formal agents of the socialization system than were social workers.

Although the contrasting means by which a decision is made to enter the specialty fields of psychiatry, clinical psychology, and psychiatric social work can, quite plausibly, be attributed to the differences in the organization of the training programs in the three disciplines, it is clearly inadequate to account for the unique pattern by which psychoanalysts arrive at the decision to specialize in psychiatry. At the point of initial choice of a professional field, psychoanalysts are virtually indistinguishable from psychiatrists in terms of the identity of influential figures, the dominant modes of influence, and the major reasons for choosing a career in medicine. However, at the second stage of choosing to specialize in psychiatry, psychoanalysts differ markedly from psychiatrists on every one of the dimensions. Specifically, peers and not professionals or teachers were the influential figures for psychoanalysts, and intellectual stimulation rather than serving as a role model was the major mode by which influence was exercised. Moreover, the influential experiences for psychoanalysts consisted of reading and working; they were not related to training. Finally, psychoanalysts were much more likely than psychiatrists to cite the desire to understand people as their reason for selecting the psychiatric specialty. In sum, psychoanalysts selected the same specialty as psychiatrists even though they rejected the very influences that psychiatrists cited as influencing their specialty choice. In view of the fact that no differences were detected in the type of professional training received by psychiatrists and psychoanalysts up to the point of choice of a specialty, this finding is indeed remarkable. Although we are unable to explore the full range of implications contained in this interprofessional discrepancy, it does seem clear that psychiatrists view the specialty much more in terms of technical skills than is the case for psychoanalysts. Conversely, we earlier presented findings suggesting that psychoanalysts, at the time of choice of a specialty, are more interested in theoretical models than are psychiatrists. Thus contained in our data is the suggestion that psychoanalysts are attracted to the specialty field of psychiatry largely by its accumulated body of theoretical knowledge, whereas psychiatrists are attracted to the specialty by its technical skill system. This explanation is plausible, but it immediately raises two questions: (1) If psychoanalysts choose psychiatry because of its theoretical structure, why do they later go on to receive additional psychoanalytic training? (2) How can psychoanalysts continue to be largely unconcerned with technical skills throughout the lengthy and intensive period of professional socialization required to become a psychiatrist? A clue to the possible answer to each of these questions is contained in the reasons cited by psychoanalysts for entering the specialty of psychoanalysis.

For psychoanalysts the most salient motive for entering psychoanalysis is to help people; approximately a third (34 per cent) of all motives discussed are so categorized. This figure is exactly double that which appears on this dimension for the earlier decision to enter psychiatry. Conversely, the frequency with which the motive to understand people is mentioned (18.4 per cent) is about half the comparable figure for the prior decision to enter psychiatry. This double reversal is striking. It clearly suggests that the decision to obtain psychoanalytic training rests more on a desire for a therapeutic technique than for a therapeutic theory.

It is also important to note the relative unimportance of the motive to understand oneself (6.8 per cent). Indeed, although a crucial part of psychoanalytic training is the trainee's own analysis, the frequency with which self-understanding is cited as a motive for entrance here is even less than when that motive was discussed in the context of entrance into psychiatry. Many psychoanalysts (and, indeed, many members of the other mental health professions) who, at the time they began their own analyses, thought they were doing so for professional reasons only report "discovering" later that personal reasons also dictated this decision. Most likely this is also true for psychoanalysts' decisions to begin analytic training.

Finally, a high proportion (39 per cent) of motivations manifested by psychoanalysts was so idiosyncratic as to preclude categorization. Our data make it clear that correlative with interests in more advanced and refined professional specialties are more varied and individualistic motivations.

When these findings are summarized, they lead to the conclusion that psychoanalysts do not remain unconcerned with technical skills throughout their professional training but, rather, postpone their commitment to psychotherapeutic techniques until the final stage of their professional socialization, that of psychoanalytic training. In fact, the decision to undergo analytic training is based essentially on the desire to acquire a particular type of technical competence. Exactly why psychoanalysts view the specialty of psychiatry primarily from a theoretical perspective and postpone commitment to technical considerations until analytic training is not clear. Quite possibly, a significant part of the explanation may reside in the social factors (cultural affiliation, religious apostasy, political liberalism) found earlier to be associated with their early acceptance of psychological determinism. In any case, it is clear that the factors relevant to explaining the differences between psychiatrists and psychoanalysts are external to the professional training systems. Thus the extent to which initial choice of an occupation can be extended to the secondary choice of a professional specialty depends on the extent to which the professional training system is formally structured and, in clearly delineated training systems, on the extent to which various social attributes of the trainees are related to the specialized role ultimately selected.

VII

Pathways to Professional Identity

The four core mental health professions under examination—psychoanalysis, psychiatry, clinical psychology, and psychiatric social work—possess related and partially overlapping functions and responsibilities and share a general societal mandate to treat mental illness. Although interrelated in many respects, the members of these four groups represent the end products of four distinct professional training systems, which vary not only in the amount and types of specialized training but also in the intensity of professional socialization that aspirants are required to undergo to obtain certification as qualified practitioners. These differences in training programs should not, however, obscure the fact that the socialization processes in all four professions have, as a major objective, the acquisititon of a distinctive set of skills in social interaction by all recruits. Blum and Rosenberg (1968) refer to these skills in social interaction as the "psychotherapeutic skill system" and designate it as "the distinctive set of skills which any presumably competent psychotherapist is expected to master." Analytically, it is divisible into three basic components (p. 74):

> First, every psychotherapist is expected to stay in psychotherapeutic "face" and cultivate "poise" in the presence of people who

> are troublesome and behavior that is unexpected. Secondly, every therapist is expected to conduct his relationship with the patient in such a way that the patient comes to be primarily regarded as an object of theoretic interest rather than an object of affective involvement. Finally, every psychiatrist is expected to develop a capacity to elicit, manage, and codify information he receives from the patient in an orderly and systematic fashion so that he may formulate rapid and accurate estimates of the patient's mind.

Although these skills in social interaction clearly do not constitute all or even most of the competencies required for certification as a professional in any of the four professions, they are basic elements in the socialization of all mental health professions. Since our examination is confined to certified practitioners in each of the four professions, we can assume that they have all mastered, in varying degrees, the basic ingredients of the psychotherapeutic skill system. Consequently, our central focus will be on the ways in which the various professional training systems are considered, by psychotherapists, to facilitate the mastery of these and related skills.

Obviously, experiences that contribute to the development of the ability to participate competently in a unique, highly specialized form of social interaction may occur in various social contexts. In recognition of this fact, we will examine the socialization of psychotherapists in two broad areas. First, we will consider the socialization experiences embodied in the formal training programs of each of the four professions. Secondly, we will investigate socialization through the experience of personal psychotherapy. The distinction between these two areas is accurately summarized by the terms "professionalization" and "professional socialization."

Professionalization

To achieve our primary objective of describing the ways in which psychotherapists respond to professional socialization pressures, it is necessary to describe briefly the formal training programs. The requirements built into these training systems produce typical trainee routes, but they are not so rigid as to prevent differences in curricula at some levels of training as well as considerable variation in sequence and length of training. There are also some differences between older and younger practitioners consequent to changes in the requirements within the systems over time. Since entrance into the professional training system begins, in many cases, during the undergraduate years, we shall begin our examination of the training of mental health professionals at that point.

Both psychiatrists and psychoanalysts were, of course, required to plan their undergraduate education to meet the requirements for admission to medical school. As a result, the majority of the members of these two professional groups had, as their undergraduate major, either biological science or the premedical curriculum. The remaining members of these two professions were divided fairly evenly among physical science, behavioral science, and the liberal arts-preprofessional curricula. These figures are presented in Table 33.

The majority of clinical psychologists and psychiatric social workers majored in one of the behavioral sciences (psychology, sociology, anthropology). Most of the remainder chose some liberal arts or preprofessional curricula, with only small numbers majoring in the physical or biological sciences.

With regard to type of institution attended for undergraduate degree, 13 per cent of the psychoanalysts and 12 per cent of the psychiatrists received their undergraduate education in foreign institutions, whereas the comparable figures for clinical psychologists and psychiatric social workers are 4 per cent each. Conversely, nearly half the clinical psychologists and psychiatric social workers received their education in public rather than private institutions; the corresponding figures for psychoanalysts and psychiatrists are slightly more than one-third. The overrepresentation of foreign-born practitioners in the two medical professions accounts, in large part, for the first pattern. The latter pattern undoubtedly reflects the lower socioeconomic background of psychologists and social workers compared to the medical professionals.

Professional Training Route for Psychiatrists and Psychoanalysts: Almost all (93 per cent) of the psychiatrists and psychoanalysts entered medical school immediately after completion of the undergraduate program. Those who did not spent some time in graduate school, taking courses in either psychology or the biological sciences. With regard to the type of medical school attended, nearly half the psychiatrists and psychoanalysts attended a private institu-

Table 33. UNDERGRADUATE MAJOR, BY PROFESSION

Undergraduate Major	PROFESSION			
	Psychoanalyst	Psychiatrist	Clinical Psychologist	Psychiatric Social Worker
	Per Cent			
Physical Science	10.9	10.9	3.0	1.6
Biological Science, Premed	63.4	67.3	5.4	2.8
Behavioral Science	12.5	10.8	66.8	70.9
Liberal Arts, Preprofessional	13.1	11.0	24.8	24.7
Total	99.9	100.0	100.0	100.0
	(503)	(576)	(1379)	(1099)

No answer = 435

$\chi^2 = 967$, $p < .01$

tion, slightly less than one-third attended a public institution, and one-fifth attended a foreign institution.

To a certain extent, the relatively high proportion of respondents attending medical school abroad reflects the fact that approximately one-quarter of the psychiatrists and psychoanalysts in our sample are foreign born. However, it should be noted that a much larger proportion of psychiatrists and psychoanalysts attended medical school abroad than attended foreign institutions to obtain their undergraduate education. Specifically, 12–13 per cent attended undergraduate school abroad and 20 per cent attended a foreign medical school. Clearly, the group attending medical school abroad is not composed solely of foreign-born practitioners who completed all their education abroad. Undoubtedly, the inability to gain entrance into medical schools in the United State contributed significantly to the number of practitioners enrolling in foreign medical schools. Although space limitation was one major factor operating to restrict medical school enrollment in this country, it must also be noted that specific restrictions have existed historically in U.S. medical schools to limit enrollment of minority-group members, particularly Jews. Thus it was a matter not of preference but of necessity that led many psychiatrists and psychoanalysts to attend foreign medical schools. Some idea of the extent to which this conclusion is warranted can be obtained by noting that, of those who did attend foreign medical schools, nearly half returned to the United States for their internship. Similarly, no more than 5 per cent of those attending foreign medical schools also took a psychiatric residency abroad.

With regard to length of time required to complete medical school, 59 per cent of the psychiatrists and 51 per cent of the psychoanalysts completed it in the standard four years. For psychiatrists the balance of the group is evenly distributed between those who finished in less than four years and those who finished in more than four years. Among psychoanalysts a somewhat larger proportion (29 per cent) finished in less than four years than in the extended period. Since the standard medical school curriculum is completed in four years, how do we account for the large number of respondents who took either more or less than this amount of time? Unfortunately, we do not have direct evidence on this issue.

However, two findings bear indirectly on the problem. First, when the psychiatrists and psychoanalysts are dichotomized at the median into two age groups, we find that almost twice as many older physicians as younger took five years or more to complete medical school. Apparently these older practitioners were educated during an era when it was quite common for a student to spend more than four years in medical school. Secondly, since most of those finishing medical school in less than four years received their education during the war years, it seems likely that our findings can be accounted for, at least in part, by the existence of various special programs in medical education during the 1940s.

Regarding medical internships, nine out of ten psychiatrists and psychoanalysts completed this training requirement at an institution in the United States. Although the vast majority of psychiatrists and psychoanalysts had a one-year internship, some practitioners (approximately 25 per cent) either took more than one internship or took an internship lasting longer than the standard period. As a result, the mean length of time spent in medical internship for both professions is 1.5 years.

Following internship the next step in the training of the medical professionals is hospital residency, which was a three-year program for almost half the psychiatrists and psychoanalysts. However, although the mean length of psychiatric residency is virtually identical for the two groups (3 years), a noticeable interprofessional difference does exist in the proportion of practitioners taking less than and more than the average time. That is, psychoanalysts have a somewhat greater tendency to finish the residency in less than three years and psychiatrists have a greater tendency to spend more than three years on a residency. To a certain extent these differences are related to the differences in length of time spent on internships. That is, since a three-year residency is required to receive certification from the American Board of Psychiatry and Neurology, it seems likely that, in many cases, individuals took two internships with one of them contributing to the fulfillment of residency requirements. It is also possible that the practitioners who spent more than three years in a psychiatric residency did so to further prepare themselves to take or retake the Board examination.

With the completion of the psychiatry residency, the formal

training program for psychoanalysts becomes differentiated from that of psychiatrists. Specifically, all psychoanalysts enter the training programs conducted by institutes approved by the American Psychoanalytic Association, but 49 per cent of the psychiatrists consider their formal training completed at the end of the psychiatric residency. Of the psychiatrists who do take postresidency training, about 30 per cent enter psychotherapy training programs conducted by approved institutes, 26 per cent enter similar programs conducted by institutes not approved by the American Psychoanalytic Association, 20 per cent enroll in therapy programs offered by universities, and the remainder receive additional training in various medical centers.

Thus the range of professional training programs is much broader for psychiatrists than for psychoanalysts. Not only does the type of training differ between the two medical groups, but, as revealed in Table 34, there is also a marked difference in the length of professional training programs. Half the psychiatrists completed their professional training in two years or less, whereas two-thirds of the psychoanalysts took five years or more to complete their psychoanalytic training. More specifically, 27 per cent of the psychiatrists completed their professional training program in one year, and 26 per cent of the psychoanalysts took seven or more years to complete the institute program. Even more striking, perhaps, are the differences in length of postresidency training that emerge when practitioner age is taken into account. When psychiatrists and psychoanalysts are dichotomized at the median age for their profession, we find that younger psychoanalysts took, on the average, 5.7 years to complete the institute program and older psychoanalysts took 5.2 years. However, no appreciable difference exists between the two groups of psychiatrists. Thus, to the extent that trends in the profession can be inferred from age grouping, the evidence suggests that length of psychoanalytic training may be increasing.

Summarizing the findings on typical training routes in the two medical professions, we find that the mean length of time in training, from undergraduate education to the completion of postresidency training, is 12.6 years for psychiatrists and 15.1 years for psychoanalysts. When we add the twelve years normally spent in elementary and secondary school, we find that psychiatrists, on the

Table 34. LENGTH OF POSTRESIDENCY TRAINING PROGRAM FOR PSYCHOANALYSTS AND PSYCHIATRISTS

Length of Post-Residency Training Program	PROFESSION	
	Psychoanalyst	Psychiatrist
	Per Cent	
One Year	1.2	27.1
Two Years	5.6	22.9
Three Years	9.6	12.3
Four Years	17.3	10.2
Five Years	20.1	9.2
Six Years	20.3	5.3
Seven Years	9.8	4.9
Eight Years	5.8	1.4
Nine Years or More	10.3	6.7
Total	100.0 (468)	100.0 (284)
Group Mean	5.4	3.3

No answer = 259
$\chi^2 = 292.48$, $p < .01$

average, are engaged in education and training programs for 24.6 years and the comparable figure for psychoanalysts is 27.1 years—a considerable proportion of the normal life-span.

Professional Training Route for Clinical Psychologists: Despite the fact that clinical psychologists were slightly more likely to attend public than private institutions to obtain their undergraduate education, a clear-cut majority (58 per cent) started their graduate program in private institutions. In fact, the proportion of clinical psychologists attending a private institution for their initial graduate work is higher than the proportion of psychiatrists and psychoanalysts attending private medical schools. Unlike physicians, however, very few clinical psychologists attended foreign institutions for graduate work.

Since clinical psychologists generally do not decide on their professional specialty until they are 26 years old, it is not surprising that, at the first graduate institution attended, 14 per cent specialized in some field other than psychology, 66 per cent specialized in some area of psychology other than clinical, and only 19 per cent specialized in the clinical program. However, the length of time spent in the first graduate institution was relatively brief, the mean being 2.7 years.

The vast majority of psychologists go on to a second graduate institution or enroll in another degree program at the same university. The proportion attending private institutions is even larger for the second than for the first graduate school (70 per cent versus 58 per cent). At this stage of their graduate program, still less than one-third (29 per cent) are formally enrolled in a clinical program but virtually all are in some branch of psychology. Since most trainees are engaged in doctoral programs by the time they enroll in the second graduate program, the length of time spent at this level rises to a mean of 4.5 years. In fact, 44 per cent spend five years or more in the second graduate program. This finding becomes extremely interesting when contrasted with our findings on the outcome of graduate school attendance: only 59 per cent of our sample of clinical psychologists fulfilled all the requirements and received their Ph.D. and 41 per cent had not completed a doctoral program. Furthermore, since only 40 psychologists are currently enrolled in a degree program, we can conclude that virtually all of the psychologists who have not received the Ph.D. no longer intend to.

Clinical internships were taken by 29 per cent of the psychologists. The internship usually occurred before the Ph.D. degree was received and lasted, on average, 2 years. However, the majority of interning psychologists (53 per cent) took a one-year internship; the remainder took internships ranging from two to eight years. However, many of these longer internships occurred during the war years and undoubtedly reflect military experience that was accepted by psychology departments as meeting the requirements of a clinical internship. The one-year internship is, of course, the standard, and the vast majority of psychologists trained since the war completed their internship in that period of time.

To obtain additional training the clinical psychologist may, upon completion of his Ph.D., enroll in a postgraduate program. This option was exercised by 34 per cent of the clinical psychologists who received their Ph.D. Most often psychologists enter postgraduate programs to obtain further training in psychotherapy, particularly psychoanalysis. In fact, of those clinical psychologists who sought post-Ph.D. training, the majority (51 per cent) attended psychoanalytic institutes in which they could become certified as "lay" psychoanalysts. However, a sizable proportion (16 per cent) of clinical psychologists elected to take postgraduate training in institutes approved by the American Psychoanalytic Association, even though they could not be certified as analysts by such institutes. Those taking postgraduate work in universities (28.9 per cent) did so primarily for the purpose of gaining additional training in psychotherapy and not for the purpose of research training. Perhaps because the emphasis is on psychotherapy, the amount of time spent by clinical psychologists in postgraduate training programs is considerable. Specifically, the mean length of postgraduate training for clinical psychologists is 3.9 years. (The range is from one year—19.4 per cent—to seven years or more—16 per cent.) Thus the average time spent by clinical psychologists in postdoctoral programs is somewhat less than the average of 5.4 years spent by psychoanalysts in institutes but slightly more than the 3.3 year average for psychiatrists in postresidency training programs. In short, although the formal training program in clinical psychology does not place so much emphasis on the performance of psychotherapy as does the training program in psychiatry, clinical psychologists who elect to take additional training at the postgraduate level receive as much, if not more, training than psychiatrists who do not enter psychoanalytic training.

In its most extended form, then, the training program for clinical psychologists ranges from the beginning of undergraduate school to the completion of postgraduate training. Approximately 31 per cent of the clinical psychologists in our sample went all the way through such a training schedule, with the mean length of time required for completion of 11.3 years. If we add the twelve years of elementary and secondary school education, we find that psychologists, on the average, have been engaged in education and training for twenty-three years.

Professional Training Route for Psychiatric Social Workers: The training route for psychiatric social workers is the shortest of any of the four mental health professions. For the majority of social workers it consists of a two-year graduate school program in social work leading to a master's degree. Despite the fact that social workers are recruited from low socioeconomic backgrounds more often than members of the other professions, they are more likely than other professionals to attend a private rather than public graduate institution. Specifically, 73 per cent of the social workers attended a private graduate school. This finding is even more surprising when it is noted that there is no difference between males and females with regard to type of graduate institution attended. Similarly, there is no sex difference in the length of time spent on the first graduate degree, although for the profession as a whole there is considerable variation around the normal two-year period required for a master's degree. In fact, the mean length of time required to obtain the master's degree is 2.4 years, with sizable proportions taking both more and less than the standard two years.

Following completion of the master's degree program, only 27 per cent of the social workers enter a second graduate program. Of the social workers who do enroll in a second program, 60 per cent do not receive a degree. Among those who do receive a degree, 57 per cent receive a Master of Social Work degree after receiving a master's degree in some other area in their first graduate program; 12 per cent receive a master's degree in one of the behavioral sciences, usually psychology; and 31 per cent receive a Ph.D. or Doctorate of Social Work. The mean length of time spent by social workers in the second graduate program is three years.

The final phase of training, postdoctoral work, is undertaken by only 17 per cent of the psychiatric social workers. The majority of psychiatric social workers (53 per cent) receive postgraduate training in universities. Although a sizable proportion of social workers do enroll in postgraduate programs conducted by psychoanalytic institutes (12.9 per cent in institutes approved by the American Psychoanalytic Association and 29.9 per cent in other institutes), they are much less likely than psychologists to receive training in such settings. Finally, psychiatric social workers who do enter institute programs tend to spend less time in the programs. Postgraduate training for psychiatric social workers averages 3.1 years (34.9 per cent take one year, 43.8 per cent take two to four years, and 21.2

per cent take five or more years). As a result, the mean overall length of training from undergraduate school to completion of postgraduate training is only 7.7 years for psychiatric social workers.

Current Training: On the basis of the average length of training programs in the mental health professions, we might expect psychotherapists to consider their formal preparation sufficient and to end their training with the completion of these lengthy programs. However, this is not the case. A sizable proportion of the membership of each profession was engaged in courses or training on a part-time basis at the time of the survey. Specifically, 41 per cent of the psychoanalysts, 32 per cent of the clinical psychologists, 29 per cent of the psychiatric social workers, and 25 per cent of the psychiatrists are currently engaged in educational and training activities. Obviously, for a large proportion of mental health professionals, training is never completed but continues hand in hand with practice.

Training Programs as Professional Socialization Systems: Having described the formally organized training programs in each of the mental health professions, it is now possible to focus on the socialization experiences contained in the programs. Specifically, we will consider the following question: of all the socialization experiences embodied in the professional training programs, which ones do "fully formed professionals" identify as having contributed significantly to the development of their present psychotherapeutic skills?

To initiate our investigation of training programs as socialization systems, the interview respondents were asked for two separate global evaluations of their formal training—one for the value of their training for their career as a whole and the other for the value of their training for their present job. Few distinctions were in fact made. Thus, in the global ratings, presented in Table 35, there are no significant differences between ratings of value for career and value for present job. There is a general tendency, however, toward lower ratings of the latter. Apparently respondents saw their training as more relevant to their career than as specifically valuable for current jobs, which were often dependent on highly specialized skills and knowledge acquired over many years of practice in the field.

Table 35. VALUE OF FORMAL TRAINING AS A WHOLE BY PROFESSION

For Career (C), for Job (J)

	Psychoanalyst		Psychiatrist		Clinical Psychologist		Psychiatric Social Worker	
	Per Cent							
	C	J	C	J	C	J	C	J
Positive	20	18	17	16	12	11	31	30
Qualified Positive	67	62	55	54	53	49	54	46
Mixed, Mainly Negative and Irrelevant	13	20	28	30	35	40	15	24
Total	100 (51)	100 (50)	100 (58)	100 (56)	100 (75)	100 (75)	100 (78)	100 (78)
Mean Rating	1.94	2.02	2.10	2.14	2.23	2.29	1.85	1.95

Although the four professional groups vary significantly in the global ratings, some generalizations can nevertheless be made about the entire sample in that they generally hold true for each of the professions. Only a minority of the total sample were willing to be unreservedly positive in their evaluations. More than half rated their training as generally positive but with some qualifying criticism, and a minority fell into the remaining categories of mixed, mainly negative, and irrelevant.

One would certainly expect that training programs devised to inculcate professional skills would be found to be valuable and relevant by the majority of mental health practitioners. At the same time, one would also expect that many professionals would find much that needed improvement and that some parts of training would be found irrelevant. What might be surprising is that approximately a fourth of the total sample raise serious and extensive objections to their professional socialization. In fact, 12 per cent of the sample consider their professional training as irrelevant for the performance of their current job and 6 per cent consider their preparation irrelevant for their entire career. Of course, the level of dissatisfaction is not uniformly high for all four professions. Specifically, social workers evaluate their formal training more highly than did the other professional groups. Psychologists were significantly lower in their evaluations, both for relevance for career and relevance for present job. If mean ratings are compared, social workers rank highest, analysts second, psychiatrists third, and psychologists lowest in the value they place on their training.

To explicate these differences between the four professions, we must anticipate some later findings. The global rating we are discussing is really a composite that the respondent has put together out of his judgments about various levels of training. They differ in number and in impact among the four professions. Two general rules seem to be operating to produce the relative ranking of social workers, analysts, and psychiatrists. First, the most recent, most specialized level tends to be seen by each profession as the most relevant. Thus social workers found that the most valuable aspects of their training occurred at the graduate level, which is for them the most recent. Analysts found the institute and internship-residency levels most important, and psychiatrists said their most significant experiences occurred at the internship-residency level. Consequently, with increasing levels of education, more levels tend to be regarded as irrelevant, and the global rating of training is thus decreased. If this rule alone were operating we would expect social workers, who are required to take the least training, to be highest, and analysts, who take the most, to be lowest.

But a further factor operates to raise the global rating given by analysts to about the same level as that given by psychiatrists. This factor is the value each profession places on this most recent, most specialized level of training. Although it is always highest relative to the other levels of training taken by that profession, there are still further differences between professions. Social workers found their graduate training more valuable than did any other profession. Analysts placed an extremely high rating on their institute training and also rated their internship-residencies much higher than did psychiatrists. Both analysts and psychiatrists would have their global ratings lowered somewhat by the inclusion of the less relevant medical school level. Psychiatrists' global ratings are further decreased below that of analysts by their lower rating of the internship-residency level of training.

What remains to be explained is the fact that psychologists are the most critical of all professional groups in their global ratings of training. Like social workers, they found their most important training experiences at the graduate level, which was the highest level of training taken by all psychologists. Some psychologists went on to take internships, but some did not. Thus the number of levels involved is somewhat more than for social workers but less than for the medically trained professions; one might expect, on the basis of this factor alone, that their global ratings would be lower than those of social workers but higher than those of analysts and psychiatrists. But more years were spent at the graduate level, much of them in what is apparently perceived to be irrelevant study, because psychologists were much more critical of graduate training than were social workers. Those who took internships tended to rate that level somewhat lower than did analysts but not lower than did the psychiatrists. Their global rating thus cannot be completely explained by number of irrelevant levels or lower ratings of the internship experience, and we must look at some other features of their training as a whole. A possible explanation lies in the academic-research tradition within psychology at the expense of more emphasis on clinical training. Furthermore, internships, for those who took them, were much shorter than the internshsips and residencies of the medically trained people. The low global rating of psychologists almost certainly reflects dissatisfaction with their less adequate clinical preparation.

Significant Training Experience: Following the general question of relevance of formal training, the interview respondents were asked specifically to evaluate the significance of didactic work, relationships with supervisors, and relationships with patients. Respondents tended to summarize all of their training experiences, highlighting those that had special significance to their overall career and to their particular job. This pattern produced a list of twenty specific training experiences that could be grouped into four general categories: intellectual or cognitive experiences, supervision, field or clinical experiences, and personal psychotherapy. The various training experiences which were mentioned as being important for career and for current job are listed in Table 36, grouped under the four general headings and arranged in order of frequency of mention. The ordering of experiences is the same for importance for career and importance for job. With the exceptions noted, no significant differences occur among the four professional groups; thus the ranking can, in a general way, be considered to characterize each profession.

Since competency in a highly specialized form of social interaction is required of all mental health professionals, it is not surprising that the types of socialization experiences most frequently mentioned as important are supervision, work experiences, contact with patients, field work, and personal psychotherapy. Each of these aspects accounts for about 10 per cent or more of the first choices of the practitioners. Similarly, since interpersonal skills are learned primarily by engaging in social interaction, it is not surprising that the specific experiences grouped under the intellectual label are less frequently seen as important.

Among the various specific experiences that are considered important by mental health professionals, supervision stands out as being the single most important experience. That this particular ex-

Table 36. Most Important Aspects of Training: Total Sample

	For Career (243)			For Job (235)		
	First Choice	Present in Three Choices	Absent in Three Choices	First Choice	Present in Three Choices	Absent in Three Choices
	Per Cent					
Clinical						
Work Experience	16	30		17	34	
Patients[a]	9	20		9	19	
Field Work, Placement[a]	13	17		10	14	
Colleagues	3	8		2	8	
Practitioners	1	4		1	3	
Staff Meetings	—	2		—	2	
Institute Orientation	1	1		—	1	
Total	43	82	18 = 100	39	81	19 = 100
Intellectual						
Formal Training	7	14		6	11	
Courses	4	13		3	11	
Faculty	7	11		6	10	
Reading	2	9		2	10	
Study Groups	2	5		2	6	
Institutes and Workshops	—	1		—	1	
Postgraduate Courses	—	1		—	—	
School's Orientation	—	—		—	2	
Total	22	54	46 = 100	19	51	49 = 100
Supervision						
Supervision	21	53	47 = 100	22	51	49 = 100
Therapy						
Personal Analysis or Therapy[a]	9	21		12	22	
Didactic Analysis or Therapy	1	4		—	3	
Total	10	25	75 = 100	12	25	75 = 100
Nothing Important	2			5		
Everything Important	2			3		
	100			100		

[a] Interprofessional differences occur and are shown in Table 37.

perience is more frequently mentioned as important than contact with patients, work experience, or field work highlights the fact that supervision is designed to bring about increased self-understanding on the part of the trainee as well as to increase his understanding of patients. Thus, since self-awareness is generally considered to be a prerequisite for the successful performance of psychotherapy, we would expect supervision to be a highly important form of professional socialization. By the same token, we would expect personal psychotherapy to be an extremely important socialization experience. It is true that personal psychotherapy was considered the most important aspect of training by about one-tenth of the group and was listed among the three most important aspects by about twice that many practitioners. However, these figures are considerably smaller than those found under supervision. It might be thought that the discrepancy between these two types of experiences may be accounted for by the fact that not all mental health professionals had the experience of personal psychotherapy. However, when the sample is restricted to practitioners who have received psychotherapy and the four general categories of experiences (clinical, intellectual, supervision, and psychotherapy) are compared, the pattern that emerges is essentially the same as that found for the sample as a whole. Even among mental health professionals who have received psychotherapy, supervision is most often considered to be the single most important socialization experience.

Thus far we have examined the training experiences of mental health professionals taken as a group. However, the training programs of the four professional groups do differ in some respects, and, as might be expected, there are corresponding differences in the way members of the four professions evaluate training experiences. Table 37 presents the interprofessional differences existing in the designation of the most important training experience.

Field work, including "placement" without further differentiation, is much more frequently mentioned by social workers than by the other three professions, both for career importance and for job importance. For more than a third of the social workers, the first assigned work in an agency setting is considered the most important aspect of training. This choice compares with less than 10 per cent for any of the other professions. Each profession has a

Table 37. Most Important Aspects of Training: by Profession

	PROFESSION							
	FOR CAREER				FOR JOB			
	Psychoanalyst	Psychiatrist	Clinical Psychologist	Social Worker	Psychoanalyst	Psychiatrist	Clinical Psychologist	Social Worker
	Per Cent							
	(243)				(235)			
Field Work, Placement	6	9	7	41	4	8	4	34
Patient Contact	29	26	20	9	28	23	16	12
	(49)	(53)	(70)	(71)	(47)	(52)	(69)	(67)
	(206)				(200)			
Personal Analysis, Respondents Who Had Therapy	31	23	30	12	23	26	31	22
Therapy, General Category (didactic and/or personal)	39	28	30	12	30	31	31	22
	(49)	(39)	(60)	(58)	(47)	(39)	(59)	(55)

general term for this kind of experience—placement, field work, clinical internship, or residency. But the other professions isolate one kind of experience from this term; social workers do not.

Psychiatrists, psychoanalysts, and psychologists are much more influenced by patient contact as a training experience than are social workers. About one-fourth of each of these professions reported learning from patients as the single most important aspect of their training, whereas only about one-tenth of the social workers indicated this experience as the most important.

Social workers single out their own psychotherapy as the most important aspect of training for their career much less frequently than do the other professions. On the other hand, social workers mention therapy as important for their job with a higher frequency—a frequency they share with the other professions. Placement experience was seen as somewhat more important for career than for present job. Career advancement thus seems to be viewed as fairly much assured by following prescribed training programs, but undergoing psychotherapy or psychoanalysis, usually after completion of formal training, is viewed as important preparation for the particular jobs in which many of these social workers now find themselves. As a socialization experience, psychotherapy functions primarily as a process for learning psychotherapeutic skills. Apparently psychiatric social workers find that the psychotherapeutic skill system is much more important for the performance of their present job than for career advancement in the profession. It is just this fact, perhaps, that sets the career of psychiatric social workers apart from those of other members of the social work profession.

Perhaps even more important than the particular differences in the way members of the four professions evaluate their training experiences is the fact that the number of interprofessional differences in the designation of the most important training experiences is small. Despite the fact that each of the four professions has its own distinctive training program, graduates of the various programs are remarkably similar in the socialization experiences they identify as being significant. The four training programs do differ considerably, however, in the level at which the most important aspects of training occurred. Table 38 shows when,

Table 38. SINGLE MOST IMPORTANT ASPECT OF TRAINING—LEVEL AT WHICH IT OCCURRED BY PROFESSION

	PROFESSION							
	Psychoanalyst		Psychiatrist		Clinical Psychologist		Psychiatric Social Worker	
	Career	Job	Career	Job	Career	Job	Career	Job
Level	Per Cent							
Graduate	15	8	10	10	59	55	87	76
Internship-Residency	39	40	76	72	21	20	—	3
Institute	41	43	5	5	4	3	—	—
Posttraining	5	9	10	13	16	22	13	21
Total	100 (41)	100 (37)	101 (42)	100 (40)	100 (63)	100 (60)	100 (69)	100 (62)

in the training sequence, the most important aspects of professional preparation occurred.

The first fact to be observed from the table is that the level at which important socialization experiences occurred tends to be the same, whether value to career as a whole or value to present job activities is used as the criterion. This result corresponds to the earlier finding that, in a general way, aspects of training important to career are the same ones deemed important to present job activities. There is one level, however, at which slight but consistent differences appear. At the posttraining level socialization experiences tend to be of slightly greater value to present job than to career. This finding is readily understandable. The mental health professional is by this time already launched on his career, and the value of further training is seen chiefly in terms of greater skill and professional competence in handling current job situations.

The second fact to be observed from Table 38 is that for each profession the level at which the most important training experiences occurred is the level that provides the most opportunity for clinical work. Psychiatrists overwhelmingly had their most important training experiences during their internship or residency. Psychoanalysts had their most important experiences during internship-residency or during their institute training. More than half the clinical psychologists had their most important experience during graduate school. It should be remembered that this phase included, for most psychologists, some clinical work. One-fifth found this experience during their internships. In view of the fact that only 54 per cent of the psychologists are known to have had internships, this level of training emerges as fairly important. Social workers' choice of levels is restricted by the shortness of their training. More than three-fourths of the social workers reported that their most important training experience occurred during graduate school.

A sizable number of practitioners stated that their single most important training experience did not occur until after completion of formal training. This number is lowest for psychoanalysts, whose formal training is the longest. It is the highest for psychologists and social workers, whose formal training is the shortest. In this context it becomes important to know that significant socialization experiences occur after the completion of formal training. Looking back over the list of important experiences, only four could have occurred at this level and were mentioned frequently enough to account for the number of professionals in the category at issue: work experience, contact with patients, supervision, and personal psychotherapy. Of these, only work experience is exclusively post-training, and it is this aspect that accounts for the frequency of mention of this level. Those professionals with the shortest clinical preparation most frequently said that it was not until they actually got out into the field that they learned how to handle patients. But even psychiatrists, with years of clinical training, sometimes found that they learned most after they began actual practice. For many mental health professionals, psychotherapeutic skills are learned, in a very real sense, by actually treating patients.

Members of the four mental health professions differ not only in the levels at which significant socialization experiences are considered to occur but also in the number of levels of training they were likely to have experienced. To further assess the impact of training experiences at various levels of training, we confined the analysis to only those who took training at each of the levels and then determined whether or not it was mentioned among the three most important experiences. The results are presented in Table 39.

First, it should be noted that the number of levels recorded for an individual does not necessarily correspond to the number of important aspects mentioned, since several of the latter could, and often did, occur at the same level. For psychiatrists the same majority mention internship-residency. Among the small group of psychiatrists who went on for institute training, almost half included it among their most important experiences.

Among psychoanalysts two levels emerge again as the most important: internship-residency and institute. In regard to medical school, it is interesting to note that nearly one-quarter included some experience at that level as important for career, but only one-tenth included it as important for current job. They seem to be giving recognition to the value of a medical degree in the process of becoming psychiatrists or psychoanalysts but do not really find medical school experiences relevant to their present practice.

When only those clinical psychologists are included who took training at the internship and institute level, these two levels emerge

Table 39. Three Most Important Aspects of Training—Levels At Which They Occurred by Profession

	PROFESSION							
	Psychoanalyst		Psychiatrist		Clinical Psychologist		Psychiatric Social Worker	
	Career	Job	Career	Job	Career	Job	Career	Job
	Per Cent and (Base Number)							
Level	(44)	(40)	(48)	(45)	(65)	(63)	(69)	(63)
Graduate								
Present	23	10	19	20	62	62	93	84
Absent	77	90	81	80	38	38	7	16
Internship-Residency	(44)	(40)	(48)	(45)	(36)	(35)	(2)	(1)
Present	57	60	75	71	53	49	—	—
Absent	43	40	25	29	47	51	100	100
Institute	(41)	(37)	(19)	(17)	(16)	(16)	(14)	(14)
Present	63	68	42	41	44	50	7	7
Absent	37	32	58	59	56	50	93	93
Posttraining	(44)	(40)	(48)	(45)	(66)	(64)	(69)	(63)
Present	11	18	15	18	21	27	38	48
Absent	89	82	85	82	79	73	62	52

as of almost equal importance to the graduate level. Since these two levels are not required for psychologists, those who undertook such training were probably more interested in the practice of psychotherapy. Hence it is understandable that they would highly value levels of training devoted largely to the development of psychotherapeutic skills.

Of interest among the psychiatric social workers is that only 7 per cent of those who had attended a psychoanalytic institute included it among their most important training experiences. On the other hand, a rather high proportion mention posttraining experiences, such as further supervision, supervisors, employers or colleagues, or actual work situations. Whatever their reasons for attending special courses for social workers at psychoanalytic institutes, the experience was not regarded as especially valuable in preparing them for either a career or a specific job.

Summarizing the findings on the levels at which significant socialization experiences are considered to have occurred, we get the distinct impression that some stages in the training programs of mental health professionals are seen to have little value. By implication, then, the findings presented thus far raise the issue of the relative efficiency of the various professional training routes leading into the mental health field. To examine these issues, we obtained practitioners' evaluations of the adequacy and relevance of professional training at the four major levels: undergraduate, graduate or medical school, internship-residency, and institute. For all levels except undergraduate, separate assessments were made for course work and clinical work.

The distinctions we have made in the stages of professional training do not, of course, apply equally to all four professions. All professionals received undergraduate training and all had course work at the graduate or medical school level. All medically trained practitioners and all social workers also had clinical work at the graduate or medical school level, but a few psychologists did not. All medically trained practitioners took internships and residencies and gave extensive assessments of their clinical work, but only a few mentioned any accompanying course work. A little more than half the psychologists took internships, which they regarded as entirely clinical. Social workers, by and large, did not take internships—their placement is regarded as clinical work at the graduate level. Training at a psychoanalytic institute, required of analysts, was also received by some psychologists (23 per cent), social workers (20 per cent), and psychiatrists (24 per cent). At this level courses and clinical work both received an equal share of comment.

Focusing first on course work, Table 40 shows how it was evaluated at the four levels of training by the sample as a whole. It should be noted that only about a fourth of the sample gave evaluations of their undergraduate training. Most of the respondents evaluated courses at the graduate or medical school level, and most of those who took institute training evaluated the courses at that level. The number responding at the internship-residency level is small because, as noted earlier, most of the people who took training at that level felt it was all clinical and did not mention formal course work.

Table 40. VALUE OF COURSE WORK AT FOUR LEVELS: TOTAL SAMPLE

	LEVEL OF EDUCATION			
	Undergraduate	Graduate or Medical School[a]	Internship-Residency	Institute
Value of Course Work	Per Cent			
Very relevant	41	25	42	56
Generally or Somewhat Relevant	27	26	16	21
Mixed	14	30	29	18
Not relevant	18	19	13	5
Total	100	100	100	100
	(73)	(206)	(31)	(68)

[a] There are interprofessional differences, but all professions do rate this level of course work lower than any other level.

Course work at the institute level was most highly valued, with more than three-quarters of the sample rating it either generally relevant or very relevant. Course work at the graduate or medical school level was least valued, with only one-half rating it generally or very relevant. It is interesting that undergraduate courses are rated higher than courses at the internship-residency or graduate level. The difference in ratings between undergraduate and internship-residency is not significant, but the difference between undergraduate and graduate level is. This finding can be understood in either of two ways. First, it is possible that the seventy-three people who elected to make a specific evaluation of undergraduate training were those who were most impressed with this level; conversely, those who did not deem it important simply did not include it in their evaluation of formal training. The second possibility is that courses at the undergraduate level were actually more highly valued because they met expectations for that level (providing liberal education or general background), whereas courses at the next two levels, more specialized and expected to deal directly with the skills and knowledge of the practicing professional, did not, in fact, adequately convey such information.

The only interprofessional difference in the value of course work occurs at the graduate level and is shown in Table 41. Social workers differ significantly from the other three professions, placing

Table 41. Interprofessional Differences Regarding Value of Course Work at Graduate or Medical School Level

Value of Course Work	PROFESSION			
	Psychoanalyst	Psychiatrist	Clinical Psychologist	Psychiatric Social Worker
	Per Cent			
Very relevant	14	24	23	32
Generally or Somewhat Relevant	28	18	22	33
Mixed	22	32	38	25
Not Relevant	36	26	17	10
Total	100 (36)	100 (38)	100 (60)	100 (72)

a relatively greater value on their graduate courses. The medically trained professionals do not find medical school courses particularly relevant. In fact, one-fourth of the psychiatrists and one-third of the psychoanalysts do not consider their medical school course work to be relevant at all. The recurrent argument that, even though these people are devoting full time to the practice of psychotherapy, their medical background is still valuable for diagnosing neurological disorders is simply not pertinent for a large proportion of the physicians. They are slightly more positive about the relevance of clinical work during medical school, but medical school is largely course work and therefore irrelevant to a sizable proportion of the medically trained therapists. Psychologists are also quite critical of their graduate training; 17 per cent find it irrelevant and less than one-half rate it generally or very relevant. The explanation is probably the same as that advanced earlier for psychologists' dissatisfaction with their overall training—the academic and research tradition with resultant underemphasis on clinical training.

In evaluating clinical work at the three relevant stages of professional training, the mental health professionals stated a wide variety of specific values that cluster around three general themes: (1) having a personal importance, offering emotional support, confidence, awareness, and self-knowledge; (2) assisting in setting goals, directions, professional standards, and attitudes; and (3) teaching skills, methods, and understanding of patients.

Clinical work, as was true for course work, was evaluated most positively at the institute level (see Table 42). There is, in fact, an increasing appreciation of clinical training as respondents attain higher levels of teaching. Almost two-thirds of the group mentioned only the positive aspects of clinical work at the graduate level; almost three-quarters of the group reported only positive aspects of clinical work during internship-residency; nine out of ten reported only positive aspects of clinical work at the institute level. It makes sense that the clinical work most valued is the training that most closely approximates the problems and situations of actual psychotherapeutic practice. It is also understandable that members of the various professions differ in their evaluation of clinical experiences at the graduate and internship-residency stages of profes-

Table 42. VALUE OF CLINICAL WORK AT THREE LEVELS

Value of Clinical Work	LEVELS OF TRAINING Graduate	Internship-Residency	Institute
		Per Cent	
Positive	65	72	91
Mixed	24	24	8
Negative	11	4	1
Total	100	100	100
	(196)	(119)	(67)

sional training. As shown in Table 43, it is again social workers who differentiate themselves from the other three professions. Graduate clinical work was their placement—the actual work in an agency setting, under supervision, but closely simulating later work experiences. They found this level extremely valuable. Also, it was the only clinical training social workers received, and there was no other level of training with which to compare it. Medically trained practitioners and psychologists found their internships and/or residencies to be generally more relevant, but among these groups the value of this level of training varies. Psychiatrists were much more critical of this training than were psychoanalysts or psychologists. The psychologists regard this level fairly positively—principally for the simple reason that the training involved was *clinical.* The interesting difference is the one between psychiatrists and psychoanalysts. Why are eight out of every ten psychoanalysts positive in their evaluation of clinical work at the internship-residency level, when only 60 per cent of the psychiatrists are similarly positive? Most psychiatric residencies have a strong psychodynamic orientation and often a strong psychoanalytic one. It may be that psychoanalysts are earlier and more fully committed to such an approach and that the dissatisfaction of psychiatrists stems from a lingering bias toward medical skills. Certainly our earlier discussion concerning the differences between medical practitioners who went on to become psychoanalysts and those who did not supports this interpretation. Similarly, support for such a difference in the orientation of psy-

Table 43. INTERPROFESSIONAL DIFFERENCES REGARDING VALUE OF CLINICAL WORK: GRADUATE OR MEDICAL SCHOOL AND INTERNSHIP-RESIDENCY LEVELS

LEVEL OF CLINICAL WORK

Graduate or Medical School Level (GM), Internship-Residency Level (IR)

Value of Clinical Work	PROFESSION						
	Psychoanalyst		Psychiatrist		Clinical Psychologist		Psychiatric Social Worker
	Per Cent						
	GM	IR	GM	IR	GM	IR	GM
Positive	57	82	50	60	57	76	81
Mixed and Negative	43	18	50	40	43	24	19
Total	100 (35)	100 (38)	100 (32)	100 (45)	100 (54)	100 (34)	100 (75)

choanalysts and psychiatrists can be found in the findings on personal psychotherapy. Although it is required of psychoanalysts, the percentage of psychiatrists who have received therapy is significantly less than that of psychologists or social workers. To the extent that undergoing personal psychotherapy testifies to a commitment to a psychodynamic approach, fewer psychiatrists have such a commitment. Consequently, they may be less satisfied with residencies that have such an orientation.

When the findings concerning formal course work and clinical work at the various stages of professional training are summarized, it is clear that clinical experiences are more highly valued than course experiences. Thus it is not surprising that, when the two dimensions of formal training are directly compared, clinical work is more positively evaluated at each level of training than course work. Specifically, at the graduate level 51 per cent of the sample positively evaluated course work and 65 per cent positively evaluated clinical work. At the internship-residency level the figures were 58 per cent positive for course work and 72 per cent positive for clinical work. Finally, at the institute level, 77 per cent positively evaluated course work; the corresponding figure for clinical work was 91 per cent. This feeling that it was really the clinical work—putting into actual practice what one has learned—that developed competence was often verbalized by practitioners. Although course work might have been recognized as basic, the clinical training was appreciated for changing a student into a practicing professional.

Of special interest is the extremely high percentage of institute graduates who claim nothing but positive gains from their clinical work at the institutes. By the time the mental health trainee reaches this point in his training, a process of mutual selection by trainee's interest and the institute's requirements has probably eliminated those who would not find the experience wholly profitable. Any mental health professional could have stopped short of this training and still secured very respectable credentials for the practice of psychotherapy. The fact that they selected to pursue this further course of study suggests that the anticipated rewards in both skill and prestige were quite high, and the nearly universal satisfaction with the program suggests that the expectations were indeed met, especially by the clinical work at the institute.

In contrast to the above finding, we noted earlier that only about two-thirds of the psychoanalysts, less than one-half of the psychiatrists and psychologists, and only 7 per cent of the social workers volunteered aspects of training at the institute level as among their most important training experiences. Except for the psychoanalysts, the high degree of satisfaction with institute training is apparently in terms of criteria different than those used for evaluating formal training as a whole. It may be that for these groups institute training is frosting on the cake. In fact, for these groups institute training appears similar to a variety of other voluntarily acquired posttraining experiences. That is, almost all mental health professionals have participated in discussion groups and staff meetings with colleagues. Similarly, more than eight out of every ten mental health professionals have taken posttraining academic work and received additional supervision beyond that formally required. In addition, half the professionals have joined informal study groups of one kind or another. Although these experiences were not rated among the most significant socialization experiences, they were clearly highly satisfying: nine out of every ten professionals considered discussion with colleagues and further supervision to be very valuable or valuable; the comparable figures for participation in informal study groups, staff meetings, and additional academic work were, in each case, above 80 per cent. With one exception—engaging in informal study groups—there were no differences among professions in the extent of participation in the various kinds of posttraining experiences. The one professional difference in posttraining experiences contrasts psychoanalysts with the other three professions and is important because it provides a possible clue to understanding the importance of these self-initiated socialization experiences. Specifically, with regard to informal study groups, 77 per cent of the psychoanalysts said they were valuable; the corresponding figure for psychiatrists was 93 per cent, for social workers 91 per cent, and for psychologists, 84 per cent. In speculating about the reasons for the differences between the two medical groups, one is led to the possibility that the informal study groups may provide for the psychiatrists something psychoanalysts got in their institute training. The interview data provide some support for such a conclusion, in the description of the topics of informal study groups. They were most frequently oriented toward study of the work of prominent psychoanalysts, philosophical systems, or specific cases and patient studies, also analytically oriented. Many of the psychiatrists and psychologists apparently used informal study groups to study some of the psychoanalytic material that psychoanalysts studied at an institute. Psychoanalysts, whose formal training is the longest and most rigorous, participated to the same extent as other professionals in these informal groups, although they found them less valuable—probably because they duplicated other parts of their professional training.

Having isolated the significant socialization experiences and located where, in the professional training sequence, the experiences were most likely to occur, we will round out our discussion of professional training by identifying the important agents of professionalization.

It turns out that those persons whose business it is to develop the professional skills of trainees are indeed the persons most frequently mentioned as making such a contribution. Named most frequently among "three most important" were teachers (65 per cent) and supervisors (60 per cent). Considerably smaller proportions of professionals mentioned another professional in practice or a colleague (35 per cent), and still fewer mentioned their own analyst or therapist (18 per cent). Finally, a few mentioned a great man (8 per cent) or a parent in the profession (2 per cent).

As would be expected, the influence of supervisors and therapists varies by profession (Table 44). Among social workers 77

Table 44. PERSONS WHO INFLUENCED PROFESSIONALIZATION

Supervisor (S), Analyst or Therapist (A), Analyst or Therapist Only by Those Who Received Therapy (AT)

Profession	Per Cent			Base Number		
	S	A	AT	S	A	AT
Psychoanalysts	53	35	36	51	51	50
Psychiatrists	46	18	27	56	56	37
Psychologists	58	22	27	76	76	64
Social Workers	77	1	2	74	74	58

per cent mentioned a supervisor or employer; only about half in the other groups identified these persons as influential. This distinction between social workers and the other professions may reflect a difference in the availability of professional models. The social worker's contact with practicing professionals is certainly more limited than that of the medically trained practitioner who participates in internships and residencies with many specialists. It is also more limited than that of most psychologists, for whom the Ph.D. serves to open a few more doors to clinical training in wider settings. Although the social worker may operate in settings with a broad range of medical and therapeutic personnel, the status differences often limit meaningful contact. It is the immediate supervisor or employer who provides for the social worker the most significant model and the primary socialization influence.

Not unexpectedly, psychoanalysts most frequently mention their own analyst as an important contributor to their professional skills and knowledge (Table 44). Psychiatrists and psychologists also frequently mentioned analysts or therapists, but only 2 per cent of the social workers did. Whatever benefits social workers received from psychotherapy—and they rated it as valuable as did the other groups—they were not in terms of greater professional abilities acquired from their therapists. Of course, social workers perform intensive psychotherapy less frequently than do the other professionals and hence rely less exclusively on specific psychotherapeutic skills in the performance of their professional roles.

Professional Socialization

Although personal psychotherapy is formally required only of psychoanalysts, it is in fact a key mechanism for personal and professional socialization in all the mental health professions. Fully 74 per cent of the entire survey sample and more than 60 per cent of each professional group have undergone psychotherapy. This uniquely intense socialization process—involving changes in attitudes, values, motivations, and identifications—has both personal and professional objectives. Thus Levinson (1967, p. 258) observes: "The socializing experience brings about changes in certain personal characteristics; these affect the student's subsequent career and are in turn affected by it."

The prevalence of personal psychotherapy among members of the mental health professions reflects the fact that most psychiatrists, clinical psychologists, and psychiatric social workers received encouragement during their professional training to enter psychotherapy. This encouragement by professional trainers is based on the assumption that psychotherapy provides the practitioner with personal insights uniquely instrumental to the development of his therapeutic skills. Viewed in this light, the intensive resocialization that psychotherapy represents both reflects and presumably results in stronger, more binding commitments to the psychotherapeutic skill system and to the psychodynamic explanatory system. Given these considerations, it is not surprising to find, in Table 45, that the extent of participation in psychotherapy varies markedly by profession.

Psychiatrists and social workers are the least likely of the four professional groups to have undergone therapy; more than one-third of each group indicate that they have not had therapy. Psychologists fall in the middle category, having had therapy more often than psychiatrists or social workers but much less frequently than psychoanalysts. Only fifteen psychoanalysts indicated that they did not undergo therapy. Since it is a requirement of the profession, this group would be those who have not yet completed their analysis.

These professional differences are, of course, consistent with the differential emphasis placed on a psychodynamic perspective in the four professional groups. Compared to psychiatry and social work, clinical psychology is closer to psychoanalysis in its emphasis on intrapsychic determinism of emotional illness and its concomitant emphasis on intrapsychic forces leading to improvement and cure. Although these same emphases exist in psychiatry and social work, they are tempered by the medical-biological model in the case of psychiatry and by the sociocommunity model in the case of social work. To the extent that the professional skills valued in psychiatry and social work are thus balanced against the weight of intrapsychic determinism, undergoing psychotherapy (for either personal or professional reasons) is clearly less relevant.

Professional membership not only affects the likelihood of having had psychotherapy but also the likelihood of having had more than one therapeutic experience. Moreover, the overall effect

Table 45. PARTICIPATION AS PATIENT IN PSYCHOTHERAPY BY PROFESSION

	Psychoanalyst		Psychiatrist		Clinical Psychologist		Psychiatric Social Worker		Total	
					Extent, Per Cent					
Have Not had Therapy	2.5		34.6		25.2		35.7		26.4	
Had Therapy:										
Once	45.2		39.4		33.5		34.1		36.6	
Twice	33.4		16.9		23.4		18.3		22.3	
Three Times	14.6	52.3	6.9	26.0	12.3	41.2	9.3	30.2	10.8	37.0
Four or More	4.3		2.2		5.5		2.6		3.9	
Total	100.0 (608)		100.0 (709)		99.9 (1443)		100.0 (1147)		100.0 (3907)	
Mean Number of Times	1.73		1.03		1.39		1.09		1.29	
					Frequency (for those who have had therapy), Per Cent					
One Time	46		60		45		53		50	
Two Times	34		26		31		28		30	
Three Times	15		11		16		15		15	
Four or More	5		3		8		4		5	
Total	100 (593)		100 (464)		100 (1079)		100 (738)		100 (2874)	
Mean Number of Times	1.774		1.573		1.863		1.696		1.755	

of professional affiliation is the same for both factors. Of those who have had therapy, psychiatrists, followed by social workers, are most likely to have had it only once, whereas psychoanalysts and psychologists are least likely to have had only one therapy experience. Psychoanalysts and psychologists are more likely to have had two therapies than are psychiatrists or social workers. Psychiatrists distinguish themselves from the other three professions by less frequently having three therapeutic experiences. Using the mean number of times in therapy (of those who have had therapy) for comparisons, psychologists have been in psychotherapy most frequently, followed by psychoanalysts, social workers, and psychiatrists. Thus, even among those practitioners who have had psychotherapy, fewer psychiatrists and social workers repeat the experience. However, although the incidence of professional socialization via psychotherapy is lower in psychiatry and social work than in the other two professions, it does not necessarily mean that the amount of socialization is less among psychiatrists and social workers. That is, psychiatrists and social workers tend to have fewer experiences in therapy, but it is quite possible that the therapeutic experiences they do have last longer and hence produce commitments to psychotherapeutic skills fully as strong as those found among psychoanalysts and clinical psychologists. The data required to assess this possibility are presented in Table 46.

For each type of experience and for total time, psychiatrists, psychologists, and social workers are virtually identical, and all three professional groups are distinguished from psychoanalysts by the shorter duration of their therapeutic experiences. This interprofessional difference is most apparent in a comparison of figures for the total mean time spent in therapy: psychoanalysts average 5.3 years, and the other three professional groups all average 4.3 years. Since psychoanalysts do not average more times in therapy (in fact, psychologists average a somewhat higher mean of therapy incidence), this greater duration of a full year is undoubtedly attributable to the form of therapy they are required to receive—namely, psychoanalysis. We can conclude, therefore, that the amount of professional socialization conducted through the psychotherapeutic process is somewhat less in psychiatry and social work than in psychoanalysis and clinical psychology.

The suggestion that the various mental health professions

Table 46. Length of Time in Therapy, by Profession

	Psychoanalyst	Psychiatrist	Clinical Psychologist	Psychiatric Social Worker	Total
			Per Cent		
			FIRST		
One Year and Less	15	28	35	32	29
Two to Five	70	56	53	56	58
Six and Over	15	16	12	12	13
Total	100	100	100	100	100
	(588)	(441)	(1027)	(710)	(2736)
Mean	3.4	2.9	2.6	2.8	2.9
			SECOND		
One Year and Less	23	29	35	37	32
Two to Five	66	63	56	56	59
Six and Over	11	8	9	7	9
Total	100	100	100	100	100
	(299)	(177)	(559)	(328)	(1363)
Mean	3.0	2.7	2.6	2.5	2.7
			THIRD		
One Year and Less	27	32	37	39	35
Two to Five	62	60	54	52	56
Six and Over	11	8	9	9	9
Total	100	100	100	100	100
	(109)	(62)	(235)	(132)	(538)
Mean	2.8	2.6	2.4	2.5	2.6
			TOTAL		
One	2	13	13	13	11
Two to Three	14	30	26	27	25
Four to Five	36	21	22	25	25
Six to Seven	48	36	39	35	39
Total	100	100	100	100	100
	(560)	(443)	(1032)	(714)	(2749)
Mean	5.3	4.3	4.3	4.3	4.5

place differential emphasis on psychotherapy as a mechanism of professional socialization raises the question of whether members of the four groups tend to undergo therapy for different reasons. There are, of course, numerous and diverse reasons why mental health professionals undergo psychotherapy. However, these reasons can be subsumed under three, admittedly crude, categories: principally for personal problems, principally for training purposes, and more or less equally for both reasons. The categories are quite general, but they clearly were meaningful to respondents. As a result, they produced interprofessional differences in reasons for entering therapy, both for initial experience and for second experience (see Table 47). Specifically, for the first therapy experience, psychoanalysts tended to enter more often for training, whereas social workers tended to enter for personal reasons. Reasons for second therapies follow roughly the same pattern as those given for first therapies, except that psychoanalysts and psychiatrists reenter therapy for reasons that are more often personal and less frequently professional than was true for their first experience.

The emphasis by psychoanalysts on exclusively professional reasons is congruous with that profession's position that experience as a patient is essential to performance as a therapist. That is, for those planning to become analysts, there is a commitment to psychotherapy (analysis) as a professional necessity—a technical requirement based on a theoretical rationale. One's ability to perform the profession's definitive task, psychoanalysis (and to understand the profession's body of knowledge), is contingent on one's being psychoanalyzed.

On the other hand, psychiatrists' greater similarity here to psychoanalysts (as contrasted with psychologists and social workers) stems from other reasons. First, in their residencies much of their training is supervised by psychiatrists who are also analysts; hence it is likely that the analytic viewpoint of the importance of psychotherapy as a socialization experience is strongly put forth and exerts some pressure on them. Second, and more important, the training of psychiatrists (whatever its ideological context) has been directed more or less exclusively toward the end of preparing them to be therapists. This situation is in contrast to the more diffuse training received by clinical psychologists and psychiatric social workers.

Table 47. Reasons for Entering Therapy

	PROFESSION				
	Psychoanalyst	Psychiatrist	Clinical Psychologist	Psychiatric Social Worker	Total
	Per Cent				
FIRST TIME					
Personal	23	38	52	73	50
Both Personal and Professional	36 } 77	39 } 62	33 } 48	24 } 27	32 } 50
Professional	41	23	15	3	18
Total	100	100	100	100	100
	(587)	(461)	(1075)	(735)	(2858)
SECOND TIME					
Personal	35	52	51	69	52
Both Personal and Professional	44	36	34	25	34
Professional	21	12	15	6	14
Total	100	100	100	100	100
	(315)	(182)	(588)	(338)	(1423)

Thus the possible professional career benefits to be derived from the therapy experience are especially relevant to psychiatrists. By implication, then, we are suggesting that psychiatrists frequently view psychotherapy as an important part of their professional training but do not share psychoanalysts' strong commitment to therapy as a unique and strategic socialization experience. Since the proposed distinction is among respondents, all of whom claimed that they entered therapy primarily for the purpose of professional training, it is impossible to document the suggested difference between psychoanalysts and psychiatrists with the survey data. However, some findings from the interview sample do provide corroborative evidence, in the form of reasons for terminating psychotherapy. These data are presented in Table 48.

Psychiatrists more frequently terminate therapy because of preset limits or external situations (moving, illness, graduation)

Table 48. Reasons for Termination of Psychotherapy

	First Therapy		Second Therapy		Third Therapy	
	Per Cent					
Limits preset	5	25	3	18	5	10
External situation	20		15		5	
Mutual decision	46		54		55	
Respondent-Initiated	20	29	20	28	30	35
Therapist-Initiated	9		8		5	
Total	100		100		100	
	(158)		(71)		(20)	

BY PROFESSION (FIRST THERAPY)

	Psychoanalyst	Psychiatrist	Clinical Psychologist	Psychiatric Social Worker
	Per Cent			
Limits preset or External situation	22	39	22	21
Mutual decision	56	47	38	46
Respondent- or Therapist-Initiated	22	14	40	33
Total	100	100	100	100
	(37)	(28)	(45)	(48)

than is true for the other professional groups. Termination for external reasons constitutes four-fifths of this category and therefore is responsible for most of this interprofessional difference. Also, psychiatrists less frequently terminate by their own or their therapist's decision. Of this combined category, respondent decisions account for twice as many terminations as therapist decisions and therefore carry the greatest weight in accounting for the lower incidence among psychiatrists. Although it may appear that the internship and residency requirements of psychiatry, as opposed to social work and clinical psychology requirements, would necessitate more moving about and thus account for this professional difference, a comparison with psychoanalysts, who are also psychiatrists responding to the same requirements, shows that this is not the case. This finding therefore seems to imply on the part of psychiatrists a lesser commitment to their therapy and less willingness to take personal responsibility for its termination. Such a lesser commitment would be consistent with the previous finding of a lower proportion of psychiatrists who enter psychotherapy. Psychiatrists not only are less likely than other mental health professionals to enter therapy but also more likely to allow it to be interrupted.

Although psychotherapy is an important mechanism of socialization in all four mental health professions, we have thus far documented important differences among the professional groups in both rates of therapy and dominant reasons for entering it. These are, of course, important dimensions of the professional socialization process. However, they indicate nothing about the consequences of psychotherapy. Since psychotherapy, as a socialization process, focuses exclusively on developing competence in psychotherapeutic skills, data on outcomes of therapy are of strategic importance. Evaluation of past therapeutic experiences is, of course, an extremely complex and demanding task. Consequently, the issue was not raised in the questionnaire and data are not available on the survey sample. However, the issue was raised in the interviews. As a result, our examination of the consequences of psychotherapy will be conducted on the interview sample. It should be noted, however, that the interview and survey instruments contained many identical items in this area and, when they are compared, the distributions are quite similar for the two samples. We may assume, therefore, that the interview findings fairly accurately reflect the larger survey sample in this general area.

As a first step in assessing the consequences of psychotherapy, we obtained a measure of the practitioner's general satisfaction with various therapeutic experiences. The results are shown in Table 49. Although one might expect an increase in satisfaction

Table 49. Evaluation of Therapy

TOTAL SAMPLE

	First Experience	Second Experience	Third Experience
		Per Cent	
Unqualifiedly Satisfied	42	32	33
Qualified Satisfaction	26	38	38
Not Satisfied	32	30	29
Total	100	100	100
	(117)	(56)	(21)

BY PROFESSION

	Psycho-analyst	Psychi-atrist	Clinical Psychol-ogist	Psychiatric Social Worker
		Per Cent		
Unqualifiedly Satisfied	36	36	46	47
Qualified Satisfaction	35	18	19	30
Not Satisfied	29	46	35	23
Total	100	100	100	100
	(28)	(22)	(37)	(30)

with successive therapies, such is not the case: there is no significant change with successive experiences in therapy. For the group as a whole, about one-third were unqualifiedly satisfied, one-third expressed qualified satisfaction, and one-third were not satisfied. We do not know how any particular individual's evaluation of second or third experiences in therapy compared with his evaluation of his first experience. But it is nevertheless of interest that even after three experiences in therapy about one-third of a group of mental health professionals who are themselves engaged in the practice of psychotherapy are not satisfied with their own personal therapy. The reasons for this lack of satisfaction are varied and are not synonymous with denial of any positive gains. Rather, they consist of general opinions that the therapy should have been better, that more problems should have been solved, or that the therapist should have been more skillful. Often, particularly after the first therapy, the lack of satisfaction reflects the respondent's feeling that more therapy is indicated; since he does go back, it cannot be construed as a lack of faith in the therapy process but rather an opinion that the therapy process has not yet given him what he wants and expects. A few examples will illustrate some of the ways in which respondents expressed this lack of satisfaction.

> The biggest thing is that there is a great reduction in the episodes of frustration and rage at home. [Why did you terminate?] I just didn't feel like going back. I still have problems. [Mentions going into therapy again.] If I go back I think I will find a new experience with a new therapist. You see, I have trouble respecting that first therapist. He was really too passive and I was fighting passivity. There is no affect with him, no relationship. I feel nothing toward him—feel like I don't know him. I don't really feel that most psychiatrists understand human behavior.

> It was a terrible time to be analyzed in that everyone was caught up in the Nazi thing. It was no time for analysis, and they should have known better. I do not really consider it to have been an analysis.

> I don't think it has alleviated any of my symptoms, but I'm not through yet.

> I think he was an example of what I would consider the wrong kind of analyst, but I did not know that at the time.

Although evaluation of therapy does not vary much with the temporal order of experiences, professional affiliation does make a difference in the degree of satisfaction derived from the initial therapeutic experience. Psychiatrists are much more likely than the other professionals to be unsatisfied with their first therapeutic experience. The reasons for this interprofessional difference are readily identified. Essentially they are contained in the evaluations of the influence of psychotherapy on the separate dimensions of personal and professional life. Thus professionals in general felt that therapy had a considerably greater influence on their personal life than on their professional life. Specifically, nearly one-third said that the influence on personal life was a major one, whereas only 14 per cent felt it was a major influence on their professional life. Approximately equal proportions rate influence on personal life (37 per cent) and professional life (41 per cent) as moderate. Finally, the proportion of respondents who rated influence on professional life as low or said there was no influence at all (45 per cent) was somewhat higher than the proportion (32 per cent) who gave such low ratings for influence on personal life. There are no interprofessional differences on either of these dimensions. Since the impact of therapy is primarily on personal life, and since psychiatrists are less committed to psychotherapy (which they enter primarily for professional training), it is understandable that they would be dissatisfied with their therapeutic experience.

Although we have specified the relationships between reasons for entering psychotherapy and influence of therapy on personal and professional life for psychiatrists, it should be noted that the relationship is a general one, not confined to any particular professional group. Specifically, of the respondents who entered therapy primarily for professional reasons, equal proportions rated personal influence and professional influence as high. Just half rated each of these influences as high, and half rated it as low. Of those who entered primarily for personal reasons, or for both personal and professional reasons, higher proportions rated personal influence as high (80 per cent) than rated professional influence as high (53 per cent). Reasons for entering psychotherapy do not seem to affect the influence therapy has on professional life. Regardless of reasons for entering, about one-half of the professionals expressing such reasons rated influence on professional life as high. But reasons for entering do have a bearing on personal life. Those practitioners who enter for personal reasons, or for both personal and professional reasons, are more likely to experience a high degree of influence on their personal lives.

Epilogue

Some mental health professionals may feel that that which makes them distinctive is to be found in the totality of their professional training. Being a psychiatrist or a social worker or a psychologist means having had the full range of training and related experience that they indeed had. No particular part of that training could safely be removed without their being somehow less than fully trained. The psychologist may claim that his research training—even his early courses in animal learning—have somehow been relevant (perhaps in molding character), and he would not want to have missed them. Some psychiatrists, engaged entirely in psychotherapy with clearly ambulatory patients, recall their medical internship with enthusiasm, feeling that the medicine they learned was somehow crucial to their training.

But the psychologist who is a psychotherapist does little research, the psychiatrist who is a psychotherapist practices no physical medicine, and the social worker engaged in therapy does not utilize knowledge of public welfare and community organization. Of course, it is still possible that these profession-specific experiences have provided for each professional some element of value beyond nostalgia, even though the core of that experience is not represented in the posttraining professional life. We have shown, however, that these professionals themselves tend to identify as crucial only those parts of their training that are, in principle, common to all the groups—that is, the direct, personalized, and clinically relevant experiences that most closely parallel the final end point, the practice of psychotherapy.

We have already noted the marked similarities of social and family background among practicing mental health professionals, regardless of the professional route they took to become a therapist. Furthermore, despite differential points of entry into professional training, and despite some widely varying experiences within particular training routes, these professionals selectively participate in the available experiences and emerge from professional training with views and skills highly similar to those of other therapists who have taken different formal routes. Within the complex of each profession, each of these groups of psychotherapists choose highly overlapping experiences and create for themselves highly similar pathways. Finally, it should also be clear that in their posttraining lives and in their professional maturity, they perform essentially the same resultant activity—psychotherapy. To some degree therapeutic styles differ from person to person. However, compared to the activities in which nontherapist members of their professions are engaged, the similarity of work style and of viewpoint among therapists is marked and sets them apart from other nonpsychiatric physicians and other nonclinical social workers or psychologists.

In this context it is important to query the social utility of having four highly organized, well-equipped, self-sufficient training pathways, each of which produces psychotherapists. Of course, these separate pathways produce other professionals who are not psychotherapists, but the point here is that the kinds of people progressively drawn into psychotherapy are highly similar. The end product is startlingly similar. Only the intervening years of expensive, highly complex training are different—different in ways that appear to have questionable relevance to the practice of psychotherapy, at least as seen by the psychotherapists themselves and as appears in the work activities of their subsequent professional lives.

It may be thought that psychotherapists coming through different routes do indeed differ from one another in ways other than those we have discussed. We have examined here only their training years and some aspects of their family and social backgrounds. In a subsequent volume we will examine two other sectors of the lives of psychotherapists: early childhood experiences and present beliefs, ideologies, and daily activities. On the basis of an extensive personal interview, and with a sample far larger and more comprehensive than any yet reported in the literature, we will show that the differences among these four groups are insignificant in such issues as relations to parents and siblings, reported sexual histories, and aspects of cognitive development. Just as psychotherapists come from highly circumscribed family constellations and have had highly similar experiences in social and religious belief systems, they appear to have had highly similar formative experiences in significant areas of personality development.

And we will examine a further crucial aspect of this "fifth profession"—their present beliefs and ideologies as they relate to mental health, and the nature of their present daily activities in professional and personal life.

These materials will make it even more apparent that the socialization pathways chosen from within these different professions of origin have produced a common man. There are differences in ideologies and in particular therapeutic activities, but they are minimal, and, far more important, they do not differ along lines of the professions of which these therapists are members. There are some fairly obvious differences between these groups, but they are differences that stem from the early membership in the profession of origin. The differences can be called upon at will if one wants to show a difference; they serve as the basis for political organization in professional associations and as the rationale for profession-specific resentment of another profession. But their relevance to the production and final character of the psychotherapist is negligible.

Appendix: Research Methods and Samples

In our efforts to study the origins and practices of members of the four core mental health professions, we used two distinct but related approaches involving different samples and different instruments. The first, intensive, approach consisted of approximately 300 interviews with mental health professionals, 100 each from Chicago, Los Angeles, and New York City. The second, extensive, approach consisted of a survey by mailed questionnaire, with the target sample of the total population of mental health professionals in the metropolitan communities of Chicago, Los Angeles, and New York City. This Appendix describes in detail the objectives and methods of both the interview and the survey.

Interview Design

The interview was designed to probe with some depth the personal histories, careers and personalities of mental health professionals. Each interview lasted for four hours (in most cases executed in two equal sessions), during which time three instruments were administered. The first involved questioning the respondent following a fifteen-page guide that covered, in an open-ended manner, the areas of vocational choice, education and professional training, work history, experience as a therapist, view of the mental health professions, family background and personal development, experience as a patient, and current personal life (spouse, children, friends, and leisure activities). This procedure usually took about three and a half hours; the final half hour was devoted to the administration of an especially designed five-card Thematic Apperception Test (TAT) and an Identity Scale (a semantic differential in format). (Analyses of the TAT and Identity Scale data will be presented in later publications.)

Because of the nature of these interviews, in terms of both the substantial time demand and the intimacy of the material requested, it was thought that the necessary cooperation could not be obtained via a random sampling approach. On the other hand, a carefully assessed stratified sampling was impossible because reliable information on the makeup of the population was, at that time, nonexistent. These practical issues would have made it very difficult for us to achieve a sample that was statistically representative of the population. However, we were prompted by choice as well as by necessity to obtain a biased sample. First, we wanted a sample whose composition would enable us to make certain comparisons we thought vital. For example, we wanted to be sure to include enough male social workers so that we could contrast them with their female colleagues. Second, we wanted to ensure that our net would be wide enough to capture at least a few examples of all of the many species of therapeutic orientation. For example, we wanted to be certain we had some Adlerians and Jungians as well as Freudians. Given the limit of 300 interviews, the sample had to be deliberately biased to achieve these ends.

The interview target sample was selected as follows. A number of highly visible, respected professionals in the fields of psychoanalysis, psychiatry, clinical psychology, and psychiatric social work in Los Angeles, Chicago, and New York City were contacted, informed of the study's purpose and nature, and asked for their assistance. These informants made up lists of potential respondents and provided us with information on them with regard to age, sex, work setting, and therapeutic orientation. In an attempt to guaran-

Table 50. TARGET INTERVIEW SAMPLE

Chicago:	(100)
Los Angeles:	(100)
New York City:	(100)
Total:	(300)

PSYCHOANALYST: (45)	PSYCHIATRIST: (105)	CLINICAL PSYCHOLOGIST: (75)	PSYCHIATRIC SOCIAL WORKER: (75)
Freudian: (27)	Freudian and other psychotherapeutic: (45)	Freudian: (39)	Freudian: (39)
pp:[a] n = 14	pp: n = 23	pp: n = 19	pp: n = 19
org:[a] n = 13	org: n = 22	org: n = 20	org: n = 20
Other-than-Freudian: (18)	Somatic-organic: (45)	Other-than-Freudian: (36)	Other-than-Freudian: (36)
pp: n = 9	pp: n = 23	pp: n = 18	pp: n = 18
org: n = 9	org: n = 22	org: n = 18	org: n = 18
	Social-community: (15)		
	pp: n = 7		
	org: n = 8		

[a] pp means exclusively or primarily in private practice; org means exclusively or primarily in organizational practice.

tee heterogeneity regarding these variables, we devised a design to guide our selections. This quota sample is shown in Table 50.

In addition to therapeutic orientation and work setting (indeed, very roughly categorized), two other considerations determined our selections: age and sex. Thus, as far as possible we attempted to fill each of the cells in Table 50 with representatives of three age groups: the "early careerists" (respondents in their thirties), the "well established" (respondents in their forties and fifties), and the "old pros" (respondents over sixty). Furthermore, we wanted at least fifteen of the social workers to be male and fifteen of each of the other three professional groups to be female.

Not surprisingly, we encountered a number of difficulties in realizing the sampling desideratum shown in Table 50. First, the information we had used for initially classifying a prospective respondent was not always correct. For example, a professional described to us as working exclusively in an institution would often be found, after the fact, to be engaged in private practice as well. Second, we occasionally found it impossible, despite the hundreds of names submitted to us, to find sufficient numbers to fill, *even potentially,* some cells—for example, those involving somatic-organic psychiatrists. Third, the exigencies inherent in the field trips, limited in time and personnel, often prevented us from adhering strictly to the design. For example, all of the four or five respondents fitting a certain cell in a particular city might respectively be on vacation, attending a convention, unavailable except when the interviewer already had another appointment, or, indeed, unwilling to participate.

Such are the realities of research. We met them as best we could, lessening or strengthening our efforts to obtain respondents of given categories according to how many or few we already had. What degree of success we attained can be seen below in Tables 51 and 52, in which the achieved interview sample is described regarding profession, therapeutic orientation, work setting, age, and sex.

What is more important than how near or far we came to realizing the target sample design is the question of how close the sample we actually obtained came to achieving our larger purpose—to ensure coverage of the full range of roles and players in the men-

Table 51. ACHIEVED INTERVIEW SAMPLE: THERAPEUTIC ORIENTATION AND WORK SETTING

Chicago: (92)
Los Angeles: (95)
New York City: (96)
Total: (283)

PSYCHOANALYST: (57)	PSYCHIATRIST: (65)	CLINICAL PSYCHOLOGIST: (80)	PSYCHIATRIC SOCIAL WORKER: (81)
Freudian: (45)	Freudian and other psychotherapeutic: (39)	Freudian: (34)	Freudian: (51)
pp: n = 26	pp: n = 22	pp: n = 16	pp: n = 9
org: n = 19	org: n = 17	org: n = 18	org: n = 42
Other-than-Freudian: (12)	Somatic-organic: (6)	Other-than-Freudian: (46)	Other-than-Freudian: (30)
pp: n = 5	pp: n = 3	pp: n = 21	pp: n = 9
org: n = 7	org: n = 3	org: n = 25	org: n = 21
	Social-community: (11)		
	pp: n = 3		
	org: n = 8		
	Eclectic and Unclassifiable:[a] (9)		
	pp: n = 2		
	org: n = 7		

[a] For these nine cases, either their therapeutic orientation was virtually equally balanced between psychotherapeutic, somatic-organic and social-community (eclectic), or the components of their avowed eclecticism were unspecified (unclassifiable).

Table 52. ACHIEVED INTERVIEW SAMPLE: SEX AND AGE

SEX	Psychoanalyst		Psychiatrist		Clinical Psychologist		Psychiatric Social Worker		Total	
	N	Per Cent	N	Per Cent	N	Per Cent	N	Per Cent	N	Per Cent
Male	45	79	58	89	61	76	35	43	199	70
Female	12	21	7	11	19	24	46	57	84	30
	57	100	65	100	80	100	81	100	283	100
AGE	N	Per Cent	N	Per Cent	N	Per Cent	N	Per Cent	N	Per Cent
Under 30	—	—	—	—	1	1	1	1	2	0.5
30–39	12	21	22	34	25	31	19	24	78	28
40–49	17	30	23	35	28	35	36	44	104	37
50–59	19	33	12	19	20	25	23	28	74	26
60–69	7	12	8	12	6	8	2	3	23	8
70 and over	2	4	—	—	—	—	—	—	2	0.5
	57	100	65	100	80	100	81	100	283	100

tal health field. In our view this aim was generally accomplished, with one major exception: the somatic-organic psychiatrist. We wanted forty-five but got only six. Two determining factors can be identified here: first, psychiatrists professing a somatic-organic therapeutic orientation are scarce; there simply are far fewer than we thought, at least in the three urban communities studied. (We have some indication that they would be found practicing with greater frequency in areas geographically beyond our sampling purview, such as in out-of-city state mental hospitals.) One index of their rarity is the unique difficulty our informants, all highly knowledgeable of their respective mental health scenes, had in suggesting prospective interviewees who would fit this category. As a consequence, we entered the field with fewer candidates than the target cell size dictated.

The second factor accounting for the dearth of somatic-organic psychiatrists was our failure to win the cooperation of many of those we had located. In this single category of respondents we encountered an identifiable resistance. Why this was so is unknown; what is clear is that, as a group, they were unsympathetic to our purpose.

With this one exception, we are satisfied that the interview sample successfully captures the main components of the diversity that characterizes the mental health professions under study.

Once the lists constituting the target samples in the three cities were prepared, the potential respondents were contacted as follows. Each received a letter inviting their participation and describing the purpose of the research, the nature of the interview, the length of time required, and the period scheduled for data collection. The letter explained that a staff member would phone to set up the pair of two-hour sessions. It also explained how they had been selected, telling them the name of the informant who had proposed them as an interview candidate. This was done for two reasons: first, to answer the natural question "Why me?" and, second, to allow the respondent to check with the informant to learn more about us from a first-hand, known source. We were, after all, asking a great deal, both in time and substance, and we wanted to facilitate the respondent's evaluation of us.

The logistics involved in gathering approximately 300 four-hour interviews in three months (100 in each city per month) with a staff of seven interviewers were formidable. A week prior to the month of interviewing, two staff members set up the appointments so that when the interviewers arrived, each had his entire month's interview timetable arranged. The scheduling of 200 two-hour sessions was a frenzied process. First of all, mental health professionals are difficult to reach at work. The fifty-minute therapeutic hour cannot be interrupted; hence, after fifty minutes of "unavailability," we would be deluged with returning calls for a ten-minute period. Secondly, our letter requesting their participation had naturally promised to schedule the sessions at their convenience to the extent of making ourselves available ". . . at any time of the day or night and at any place. . . ." This often necessitated elaborate arrangements concerning time and place, not infrequently including lengthy directions as to how to get on and off the appropriate freeway. Third, with a limited staff, we could only accommodate a given number of preferences for the same time spot; this inability to oblige the respondent's first choice led to a further proliferation of telephoning and an ever more complicated interviewing calendar. Finally, the overall schedule, once set, did not of course remain so; changes had to be made constantly.

Let us say immediately that our respondents showed patient understanding of our scheduling difficulties. They met us more than halfway, often greatly inconveniencing themselves to fit appointments into the time slots we still had open. And this initial consideration accurately presaged the cooperation extended by the respondents with regard to the interview itself. It is not easy to give up four hours, it is more difficult still to give four hours of personal revelation. But, with rare exceptions, the respondents made a total and committed effort to make a rich and genuine contribution. When difficulties were encountered (the recollection of a painful memory, embarrassment, or even fear), the consequent unwillingness to continue was involuntary in nature and immediately overcome by a conscious effort not to withhold. About three-quarters of the interviews took place in the respondents' offices during work hours. The others were held in a variety of locales, mostly homes but ranging from bars to hospital bedsides to sailboats.

From the interviewers' point of view, the interviews were fascinating experiences; from the study's perspective, they yielded a rich harvest. Did the respondents get anything from them other than the rather abstract satisfaction of having made a contribution to research? Many of them expressed gratitude to us for structuring a process through which, unanticipated, they gained a sense of perspective on their lives and work. They recognized patterns, made connections, reevaluated experiences—in a word, made a further discovery of self that they deemed valuable. We were often in the astonished position of being thanked for having interviewed them.

The question arises as to who would not participate as an interviewee. This question is difficult to answer because, although overt refusals were rare, it is impossible to distinguish between false and genuine regrets due to lack of time, conflicting schedules, illness, and so on. However, it is our *impression* that most of those professionals who could not see us could not, in fact, for legitimate (from our point of view) reasons.

In addition to a willing and able subject, a good interview is the result of a talented and skilled interviewer. This study has been fortunate in the quality of its staff. The core group of interviewers, for all three cities, consisted of a psychologist, a sociologist, and three doctoral candidates from The Committee on Human Development of The University of Chicago. All five of this group had had extensive interviewing experience. This permanent staff was augmented in the several cities by three or four part-time people (social workers, graduate students, professional interviewers) who again came to us experienced.

Naturally, any research involving the interview as a method of data collection benefits from highly skilled and knowledgeable interviewers. However, for three reasons they were crucial to this study. First, the psychological sophistication of our respondents demanded that the interviewer himself be sufficiently sophisticated to assure the respondent that he was being understood. Like anyone else, mental health professionals want an understanding as well as a sympathetic listener; but to be such with *this* sample required considerable psychological knowledge on the part of the interviewer. Every profession has its unique vernacular, but that of the mental health professions happens to overlap with that of psychological research; thus our subjects, more than other groups, expected the interviewers to understand them literally on their terms.

The particular method used to record interviews constituted the second major demand on our interviewers' skill. In the planning of the study we had been advised by our contacts in the mental health field *not* to tape the interview sessions; such a procedure was thought to act as an inhibiting force. Consequently, the interviews were recorded as follows: extensive notes were taken (in fact, much of what was said was taken down verbatim); immediately following the session, the interviewer dictated onto tape his reconstruction of the interview. It is difficult to estimate how much is lost in this process. Certainly something of what is said is missed (as is, of course, *how* it is said). This anticipated but unknown quantity had to be balanced against the equally anticipated and unknown loss that taping would produce. At any rate, it is clear that the feasibility of such a method of recording depends on confidence in the skill of the interviewers.

A third demand on the ability of our interviewers came from our particular use of the interview schedule. This fifteen page guide contained 132 questions covering a dozen major areas of the respondent's personal life and work. Even with four hours available, we knew from our trial interviews that it would not always be possible to cover the entire guide with the desired depth. At the same time we were reluctant to further cut the guide, which was already greatly reduced in scope from what we had originally wanted to encompass. As an alternative, we decided to let the interviewers determine how much of the guide would be covered. They were to decide when an area had been sufficiently explored and hence when to go on; and, if the pressure of time required that only several of many remaining areas be covered, the interviewers, on the basis of what had already taken place in the session, were to choose which of them should be discussed. Such decisions required of the interviewer both a continuous evaluation of the material he was getting and a continuous assessment of the respondent himself.

This method of interviewing reflected our choice of "accounting"; we thought it more desirable to cover fewer areas deeply than more areas superficially. This choice was difficult to make, for it meant that for many questions covered by the interview our sample was reduced. We think our choice here was congruent with the aim that dictated the selection of the interview sample—namely, a desire for heterogeneity and coverage—but here in terms of what was meaningful to the respondents. For, although the interviewers directed the discussions, they in turn were guided to a considerable degree by what the respondent offered. What the interviews covered, then, was in part dictated by what we, the investigators, thought important. But it was also, in part, a fishing expedition, wherein the respondents placed into our gathering nets what they thought important.

In keeping with this emphasis on the respondent's freedom to offer what he thought relevant (within the broad limits set by the guide), the interview data were coded inductively. We wanted to be sure that we knew what the *respondents* said *before* we began to speculate as to the meaning of what they said. We were careful, therefore, to avoid early imposition on the data of any preconceived schemas of interpretation. Each staff member was assigned certain areas of questioning and, using a minimum of fifty random cases, established inductive codes. Of course, any process of categorizing data involves by definition some degree of interpretation; some decision as to the data's meaning is necessitated by putting two different responses, however subtle that difference may be, into the same box. The point here is that we made every effort to keep the interpretation involved in the initial coding to a minimum, anticipating that we could always later collapse coding categories and move to higher levels of abstraction when it was necessary for analysis.

Once the codes for an area of questioning had been drafted, copies were distributed to the entire staff and conferences held during which everyone could suggest modifications or additions to the codes based on their own study of the interviews. Most important, this process allowed the codes to be evaluated and changed by the interviewers in the light of their first-hand experience. This procedure, then, was a further effort at keeping the analysis close to the data.

In most cases the major part of the actual coding of any given area of the interview data was done by the person who had established those particular codes. Checking the reliability of his coding was a standard procedure. The completion of such coding constituted the basic step in the preparation of the interview data for analysis. The extent to which the data were further manipulated depended on the problems confronted in any particular area of analysis. These manipulations are specified in the context of the particular issue being discussed.

In analyzing the interview data for differences between the four mental health professions, a probability level of .10 was used. This less-than-usual stringency seems to us more appropriate to the size of the interview sample, the nature of the interview data, and the intent of the study's analysis, which is heuristic rather than demonstrative, involving the building of hypotheses rather than the testing of them.

Of course, in determining interprofessional differences, other factors had to be controlled. For example, what appeared to be a professional difference between social workers as opposed to analysts, psychiatrists, and psychologists might in fact be a sex difference determined by the significantly higher proportion of women in social work. Thus we conducted our examination of professional differences holding constant such variables as sex, age, and social class origins.

Unfortunately, the small sample size permitted us to control for only *one factor at a time*—sex, *or* age *or* social class origins. Thus we are unable to consider the interactional effect of these variables as they might relate to professional differences.

Our procedure, then, for arriving at interprofessional differences was as follows. First, the data were broken simply by the four professions and those differences that were statistically significant at the .10 level were noted. Second, a series of interprofessional runs was made, holding constant, separately, such factors as sex and age.

In deciding whether a professional difference "held up," our liberal policy was guided by the desire to avoid throwing out the baby with the bath water or—to put it positively—the desire to include those data that would point out *probable* differences between the professions. Accordingly, we decided that if the majority of comparisons were in the same direction as the original professional difference *and* if no one of them was significantly in the opposite direction, we would report and discuss the difference as a *professional* one, although noting the exceptions. In our judgment this position is reasonable in the context of the interview sample size.

The Survey Design and Sample

The questionnaire survey was designed to investigate the full range and diversity of roles, interests, and settings characterizing the professional component of the mental health field in three metropolitan communities. In addition to the fact that mental health practitioners are concentrated in and around metropolitan areas, there is a further rationale involved in deciding to select from geographic clusters rather than attempting to sample the national professional population. This rationale is based on the assumption that the metropolitan community forms the "basic" or "natural" population unit in modern society (Gras, 1922; McKenzie, 1933; Bogue, 1950). For our purposes it is possible to consider this unit as an autonomously functioning "service area" covering the variety of personnel and facilities utilized in treating mental illness. The characteristics of this basic unit thus provide the investigator with the diversity of activities that occur within the professions as a whole. Moreover, the metropolitan community provides a microcosmic representation of the mental health field, which allows us to examine the relations between, as well as within, the professions. The sample unit in each case was therefore defined as the central city and its immediate suburbs, and this unit was designated the metropolitan community. To ensure that the widest range of professional activities would be represented, the three largest communities in the nation, New York City, Los Angeles, and Chicago, were selected for study. To further ensure comprehensive coverage, questionnaires were sent to the total population of professional therapists working in the three metropolitan communities.

For purposes of the survey the Chicago metropolitan community was defined as the area referred to as the Chicago Standard Metropolitan Statistical Area and the Gary–Hammond–East Chicago Standard Metropolitan Statistical Area in the 1960 U.S. Census. The Los Angeles metropolitan community consists of Los Angeles County, which contains within it the Los Angeles–Long Beach

Standard Metropolitan Statistical Area. Finally, the New York metropolitan community consists of Manhattan and the four adjoining boroughs.

The target population receiving questionnaires in each of the metropolitan communities consisted of all psychoanalysts, psychiatrists, clinical psychologists, and psychiatric social workers involved in treating mental illness. (It is important to note that the focus of the study is exclusively on the four core mental health professions and not on mental health practitioners in general. Excluded from consideration are those practitioners who do not belong to the three major professions but do engage in therapeutic activities or actually treat the mentally ill. Examples of personnel excluded from consideration include general medical practitioners, ministers, psychiatric nurses, psychiatric aides, and nonprofessionally trained "therapists" and "counselors.") Enumeration of these practitioners was accomplished through the use of professional directories. Specifically, for psychiatrists the 1963 edition of the *Biographical Directory of Fellows and Members of the American Psychiatric Association* was used. This directory also provided information on those psychiatrists who had graduated from or were currently attending a psychoanalytic institute recognized by the American Psychoanalytic Association. (Throughout the study the term *psychoanalyst* will refer only to those psychiatrists who have attended or are currently attending a psychoanalytic institute recognized by the American Psychoanalytic Association. Professionals who had received or were receiving psychoanalytic training in organizations not recognized by the American Psychoanalytic Association (William Alanson White Institute of Psychiatry, Psychoanalysis and Psychology, The Alfred Adler Institute, National Psychological Association for Psychoanalysis) were classified according to their general professional affiliation and not as psychoanalysts.) Since both prior research and official professional statements indicate that psychoanalysts constitute a separate subspecialty in the mental health field, they were treated as a separate professional group (Strauss et al., 1964). *The 1964 edition of the *American Psychological Asso-*

* Representative of official pronouncements on the differences between the two groups is the following statement by a former president of the American Psychiatric Association: "The only true specialty inside the

ciation Directory was used to obtain the population of psychologists. Those who listed as "interests" in their autobiographical sketches in the *Directory* any of the areas concerned with mental health were included in the sample of clinical psychologists. (The specific interests defined as being concerned with mental health included psychotherapy, counseling and guidance, evaluation psychotherapy, play therapy, psychodrama, hypnodrama, family therapy, psychotherapeutic technique, marriage and family therapy, psychological counseling, nondirective counseling, and clinical psychology.) As a supplement to this directory the most recent directories of organizations composed of clinical psychologists interested in and/or practicing psychotherapy were checked. (These organizations were Psychologists Interested in the Advancement of Psychotherapy, Psychologists in Private Practice, and The American Academy of Psychotherapists. In general these directories provided very few names of psychologists not already selected from the *Directory of the American Psychological Association.* This check provided limited reassurance that the primary criterion used for selecting clinical psychologists involved in treatment—mentioning any of the above interests in the APA *Directory*—possessed validity.)

For psychiatric social workers the sources used to define the population varied by city. For Chicago and Los Angeles the *Directory of Professional Social Workers* existing at the time of the surveys (1964–1965) could not be used because it was outdated. However, it was possible to obtain lists of persons classified as "qualified, experienced" psychiatric social workers from the local chapters of the National Association of Social Workers in the geographic areas comprising the two metropolitan communities. A few additional names were secured from the 1964 *Directory of Professional Social Workers in Private Practice.* In New York City it was impossible to secure lists of psychiatric social workers from the local chapter. This made it necessary to use the 1966 *Directory of Professional Social Workers,* which was published immediately prior to the survey in New York City. The actual selection of psychiatric social workers from the directory listing of all social workers in New York

general field of psychiatry is psychoanalysis. It has a body of knowledge, criteria for selection and training of its candidates, institutes to carry out training and a method of certification" (quoted in Blain, 1953).

City was conducted in two stages. First, all social workers in the New York metropolitan community who indicated in the directory that they had received a degree in psychiatric social work were included in the list. Second, all social workers who were listed as being in private practice or as working in settings classified as mental health agencies in the *Directory of Social and Health Agencies of New York City 1965–66* were included in the population of psychiatric social workers. (This *Directory* lists facilities classified according to function. Under the general category of "mental health" the directory lists the following types of facilities: agency services, clinics for the general public, aftercare clinics of the State Department of Mental Hygiene, hospitals for mental disorders, retarded children and adults, alcoholism, and narcotic addiction.)

Using type of work setting as one of the criteria for defining the population of psychiatric social workers in New York City was necessitated by the fact that in 1955 the various specialized organizations, including the American Association of Psychiatric Social Workers, merged to form the National Association of Social Workers (NASW). The formation of one professional association resulted in the abolition of specialty degrees, including that of psychiatric social work. Hence all graduates of schools of social work after that date are simply listed in the professional directory as having an M.S.W. The standardization of the degree awarded reflects the fact that all students take the same core courses in schools of social work. However, students can still specialize in psychiatric social work by electing to take their fieldwork placement in a psychiatric setting and by taking methodology courses in psychotherapy, group therapy, and related topics. Thus psychiatric social work is still a specialty in social work training, even though it is no longer a field in which a degree may be obtained. Given this fact, it was necessary to take into account both type of degree and work setting of social workers in New York City in order to most closely approximate the lists of "qualified, experienced" psychiatric social workers provided by the local chapters of the NASW in the other two metropolitan communities. The procedure used in New York City did, however, result in our contacting a number of social workers who were neither qualified nor working as psychiatric social workers.

When evidence to this effect was obtained from respondents, either through correspondence or from the returned questionnaire, they were dropped from the population. As a result of this process it seems safe to conclude that the samples of psychiatric social workers in the three metropolitan communities were roughly equivalent.

Considered from the perspective of metropolitan mental health communities, Chicago, Los Angeles, and New York City generally resemble one another in certain respects. For example, nonmedical professional practitioners in all three metropolitan communities have only recently come under the control of state licensing standards. Similarly, the relatively recent growth of the professional mental health field has meant that the patterns of professional training and accreditation have only recently become formalized in training centers in each of the cities. The emergence over the past three decades of dynamic, intensive psychotherapy as the dominant therapeutic orientation has also had a strong impact on all three communities. Finally, all three cities have been affected by the increasing emphasis on community mental health and related programs.

More important than the general similarities between the three metropolitan communities are the marked differences between them. These differences range from general characteristics such as size and religious composition of the population to specific differences between training programs and adherence to various therapeutic orientations. Thus New York City is unique among the cities in the size of its Jewish population, whereas Chicago holds a similar position in terms of the proportion of Catholics in the metropolitan population. Similarly, the states of New York and California both have much larger budgets for mental health programs than is true for Illinois; hence we would expect New York City and Los Angeles to have many more professionals involved in community mental health and related programs than does Chicago.

With regard to professional training and treatment orientations, several factors make Chicago unique among the three metropolitan communities. One such factor is that Chicago possesses only one Institute for Psychoanalysis; Los Angeles has two and New York City three recognized institutes. That institute is the sole repository of authorized psychoanalytic training and certification in the Chicago metropolitan community. This undoubtedly contributes to a far more homogeneous ideological environment in Chicago compared to the other two cities. The existence of only one recognized institute also means that fewer psychoanalysts are being trained in Chicago than is true of the other two communities. Moreover, since psychoanalysts tend to remain in the city where they received their analytic training, this means that the psychoanalyst-population ratio is smaller in Chicago than in either Los Angeles or New York City.

Another unique feature of the professional mental health training situation in Chicago that affects the distribution of therapeutic orientations held by practitioners is the prominent position of the Counseling and Psychotherapy Research Center of the University of Chicago. Founded in 1945 by Carl Rogers, the Counseling Center has since been devoted to the application of the Rogerian approach to the problem of emotional disturbance. A large number of clinical psychologists practicing in Chicago have received at least part of their training at the Counseling Center. Thus the proportion of mental health professionals committed to a Rogerian approach is much greater in Chicago than in Los Angeles and New York City. These factors also indicate that the Rogerian orientation is primarily restricted to one professional group, clinical psychologists.

Although Chicago is unique by virtue of its homogeneity in training and ideological climate, New York City is set apart from the other communities by its unmatched diversity. Specifically, New York City not only has three psychoanalytic institutes recognized by the American Psychoanalytic Association but it also has a larger number of other postgraduate institutes, each specializing in one or another of the various therapeutic schools in the mental health field. Thus, for example, the following are some of the institutes located in New York City: The Training Institute of the National Association for Psychoanalysis (Reikian in orientation), The Alfred Adler Institute, The William Alanson White Institute of Psychiatry, Psychoanalysis and Psychology (Sullivanian orientation), and the American Institute for Psychoanalysis (Horney approach). While the other two cities have representatives of the various approaches, New York City is unique in that it has a large number of divergent camps strongly supported through formally organized centers. Moreover, if, as Strauss et al. (1964) found in their study of Chicago, major cleavages in the professional mental health field follow ideological lines then the competition and conflict characterizing the field should be most clearly revealed in New York City.

Perhaps even more important than the variety of therapeutic ideologies represented in the training centers in New York City is the fact that many of the postgraduate institutes accept candidates who do not have medical degrees. This means that clinical psychologists and psychiatric social workers in New York City have a much greater opportunity to obtain postgraduate training in psychotherapy than is true in Chicago and Los Angeles. As a result of the greater training opportunities, New York City should have a larger proportion of clinical psychologists and psychiatric social workers in private practice, either on a part-time basis or full time as lay analysts.

Most of the factors that differentiate Los Angeles from the other two metropolitan communities seem to revolve around its frontier character. Los Angeles was the last of the three cities to establish a psychoanalytic institute, and this founding occurred only after the psychoanalytic movement was well established in this country. The rapid growth in population and the subsequent demand for mental health practitioners have resulted in Los Angeles having a larger proportion of psychotherapists trained in other areas of the country than is true for either Chicago or New York City. These factors have resulted in Los Angeles' practitioners being less influenced by established training centers than are practitioners in the other cities. This fact, combined with the sprawling nature of the urban area, partially accounts for the high incidence of innovative and experimental mental health practices in Los Angeles.

On the basis of this brief outline of the mental health field in three cities, it seems clear that there is no typical mental health community. Certainly none of the three metropolitan communities studied can be used as a basis for making generalizations about the distribution of professional therapeutic activities in the other two. However, it is also clear that the differences between the three mental health communities follow a general pattern and are not simply random. Specifically, in terms of the variability of professional training and practices, the three metropolitan communities can be broadly thought of as forming two different but related continua. The first continuum refers to the distribution of professional personnel and training facilities. Chicago, being the most homogeneous of the three communities in terms of training and professional composition, would be at one end of the continuum; the heterogeneity of New York City places it at the other end. The second continuum refers to the amount of innovation or traditionalism represented in professional practices. Using this criterion, Chicago is clearly the most traditional and Los Angeles is the most innovative. Here New York City would be in between the other two cities but probably closer to Los Angeles than to Chicago. In any case, the three cities, taken together, contain a wide range of mental health characteristics. Since the objective of the study was to investigate the full range of professional activities in the mental health field, these three mental health communities seem ideally suited for that purpose.

The focus of the questionnaire was on five general areas of professional characteristics and behavior. The first area concentrated on the personal and sociocultural characteristics, past and present, of the practitioners. A second area dealt with formal and informal professional education and training as well as organizational affiliations and professional activities of the practitioners. The third area focused on the social structural matrix of professional behavior in the mental health field; questionnaire items in this section were designed to obtain information on career lines, role structures, work history, and settings in which therapists practice. The fourth area was designed to assess the therapeutic ideologies of mental health practitioners from a variety of perspectives. The fifth and final area was composed of a series of questions about the various characteristics of therapists' patients.

The questionnaire made many demands on the practitioners. It was comprehensive in its coverage of the professional field and hence required a long period of time to complete. It was also unusual in that the density of information requested in the various areas approximated the kind of data gathered in interviews rather than questionnaires. Specifically, many sensitive areas, such as marital history, respondents' own experiences in therapy, characteristics of patients, and professional fees and income, were explored intensively. Normally questions of this type are only thought appropriate for semistructured interviews. Thus, in completing the questionnaire, the respondent not only gave us at least an hour of his time but also answered questions requiring considerable thought about issues normally considered private, either in the professional or personal sense. In sum, the questionnaire contained the basis for many different types of refusals by the mental health professionals contacted. However, it also contained many interesting questions on topics considered to be important to practitioners in the field.

The questionnaire was sent to all psychiatrists, clinical psychologists and psychiatric social workers identified by the sampling procedures. Four attempts were made to obtain questionnaires from members of the target population in each community. These attempts included two mailings with accompanying cover letters, a telephone contact with those who had not returned the questionnaire after the second mailing, and, finally, a postal reminder to those who, when contacted by telephone, had agreed to return the questionnaire but had failed to do so after three weeks.

The return rates for each profession in each of the metropolitan communities are presented in Table 53. Response to the survey was much better in Chicago and Los Angeles than in New York City. There are undoubtedly many reasons for the lower return rates in New York City, but the major factors appear to be related to the field work itself rather than to characteristics of the practitioners. Thus the large size of the professional population in New York City made it impossible for us to spend as much time as we did in the other two cities in trying to contact each respondent. As a result, a larger proportion of New York City psychotherapists were not contacted by telephone than was true in either Los Angeles or Chicago. The difficulty in locating respondents in New York City means that we probably incorrectly left more practitioners in the population than was true in the other cities. Also, during the course of the field work we discovered that there were four other studies also sending questionnaires to New York City psychiatrists and psychoanalysts. Finally, during the field work it became apparent that respondents in New York City were less familiar with the personnel of the staff and with the University of Chicago than was true in Los Angeles. This was particularly true of the large number of medically trained psychotherapists in private practice in New York City who were unable to check the legitimacy of the study with knowledgeable colleagues.

Table 53. QUESTIONNAIRE SURVEY: RETURN RATES[a]

Profession	CITY Chicago	Los Angeles	New York City	Total
	Per Cent and (Base Number)			
Psychoanalysts	63.1	68.9	48.5	54.5
	(103) / (168)	(166) / (241)	(369) / (761)	(638) / (1170)
Psychiatrists	57.2	50.8	40.9	46.3
	(151) / (264)	(214) / (421)	(368) / (899)	(733) / (1584)
Clinical Psychologists	77.2	71.9	62.1	67.1
	(268) / (347)	(417) / (580)	(780) / (1256)	(1465) / (2183)
Psychiatric Social Workers	78.0	75.1	64.1	68.2
	(213) / (273)	(217) / (289)	(724) / (1130)	(1154) / (1692)
Total	69.9	66.2	55.4	60.2
	(735) / (1052)	(1014) / (1531)	(2241) / (4046)	(3990) / (6629)

[a] The percentages in the table represent the proportion of all questionnaires sent to a given profession in a given city that were returned. For example, in Chicago 168 questionnaires were sent to psychoanalysts; 103, or 63.1 per cent, of them were completed and returned.

Although New York City differs in aggregate return rate it should be noted that the order of return from the four professional groups is similar in each of the cities. In each case the two non-medical professions returned the questionnaire at a higher rate than did the medical professionals. A combination of factors seem to account for this difference between the return rates of the two groups. First, the medical groups have a larger proportion of members in private practice than is true for either clinical psychology or psychiatric social work. If we assume that private practitioners are generally less familiar with and interested in research than their institutionally affiliated colleagues, then we would expect them to feel less compelled to participate in the study. Also, being high-status professionals and the elite of the mental health field probably results in the medical practitioners' having less available time as well as less inclination to participate in research conducted by academicians. Finally, it is possible that both psychiatrists and psychoanalysts are, in general, more strongly committed to intensive case studies than the other professionals and hence less willing to participate in a survey study.

A second uniform pattern revealed in Table 53 is that in each metropolitan community the lowest response was obtained from psychiatrists, with psychoanalysts being much more likely to return the questionnaire than their medical colleagues. If we consider the difference in the training received by psychiatrists and psychoanalysts, it becomes possible to offer a tentative explanation of the differential participation of these two groups in the research. Briefly, the additional psychological training received by psychoanalysts results in their having closer ties with the academic community and hence being more receptive to research on social and psychological issues. If this is true, then their additional psychoanalytic training would lead them to respond to the questionnaire differently from psychiatrists and in the direction of being similar to the nonmedical professions. This, of course, is precisely what they do. As a result, the greatest weakness in the study, as revealed in Table 53, is the extent to which psychiatrists are underrepresented, both in the aggregate return and in the response from each city.

The telephone contact not only increased the questionnaire returns but also provided information on reasons for not participating in the study. Although the reasons individuals gave for not returning the questionnaire were not analyzed systematically for the three metropolitan communities, an attempt was made to isolate the dominant refusal themes.

One main category of refusals was composed of individuals who, when contacted by telephone, promised to return the completed questionnaire but never did. This category of unfulfilled promises to return accounted for about one-third of the population of nonreturns. Within this category psychiatrists were by far the largest professional group. Another one-third of the nonreturns consisted of practitioners who either could not be contacted or who were contacted but gave no specific reason for not participating.

Psychoanalysts made up the largest proportion of this latter group who did not feel compelled to complete the questionnaire and could not be persuaded to explain the reasons for not participating in the study. The two nonmedical professions contributed heavily to the category of those who could not be contacted. For the remaining one-third of the nonreturns the specific reasons for refusing to participate in the study fall into four categories. The most frequent reason for not returning the questionnaire involved pressures of time (which were undoubtedly felt by all practitioners contacted). Psychiatrists in particular claimed that they were just too busy, that the questionnaire was too long, that there were so many other demands made on their schedule, and that they received too many questionnaires. The next most frequent specific reason for refusing to complete the questionnaire involved the feeling that it was too personal in the information it sought. Very frequently this reason was linked to distrust of the confidentiality with which the information would be treated. Finally, some individuals in this category (which was dominated by psychiatrists) felt that the questionnaire represented a direct invasion of professional privacy and were, furthermore, indignant over the additional attempt to persuade them to fill out the questionnaire.

Although psychiatrists represented the majority of respondents in both of the first two categories of specific refusals, with psychoanalysts intermediate between them and the nonmedical professions, a higher proportion of psychoanalysts than psychiatrists refused to participate on the ground that they were opposed to the research. This was most often explained as opposition to research using this method on this particular subject matter and undoubtedly reflects their preference for intensive case studies.

The other category containing individuals who gave specific reasons for refusing to participate in the study includes a range of idiosyncratic rationales not dominated by any single theme. Moreover, this category was small and the four professional groups were fairly equally represented in it.

Since the survey was conducted on the total population of mental health practitioners in Chicago, Los Angeles, and New York City, it is important to assess the extent to which the sample of returns is representative of the population in each of the communities. In an attempt to achieve this objective, we compared the sample of returns with the target population using data drawn from the professional directories used to enumerate the professional population. Unfortunately, data on the entire target population are of variable quality; the information on psychiatrists, psychoanalysts, and clinical psychologists is the most reliable and recent and the information on psychiatric social workers is the least complete. Bearing in mind the limitations of the data, it still seems useful to compare the survey sample and the target population on the few available basic characteristics.

The first basic consideration is simply the extent to which the professional composition of the sample reflects the composition of the population in each metropolitan community. Table 54 provides the evidence relevant to this issue.

As Table 54 indicates, the greatest discrepancy appears for psychiatrists with the proportion of practitioners in the population being significantly greater than the proportion in the sample in each of the communities. The discrepancy in the proportion of psychiatrists in the sample and in the population is greatest in New York City; Los Angeles has the second greatest difference and Chicago the least difference. This, of course, is the same as the order of overall return from the three cities. Although the difference in aggregate return rates among the cities was not determined solely by the differential return from psychiatrists, it is true that the lower the city rate of return, the greater the difficulty in getting psychiarists to return. Since there is very little difference between the proportion of psychoanalysts in the sample and in the population in each of the communities, we are led to conclude that the discrepancy noted for psychiatrists is due to their unique characteristics rather than a factor common to all medically trained psychotherapists. As indicated earlier, the general factor that sets psychiatrists apart from the other groups is their greater emphasis on a medical approach to mental illness. Using this reasoning, we are led to conclude that the relatively large discrepancy in the proportion of psychiatrists in the sample and in the population in New York City can be accounted for, in part, by the fact that it is the community with

Table 54. COMPARISON OF PROFESSIONAL COMPOSITION OF SAMPLE AND POPULATION

	Chicago		Los Angeles		New York City		Total	
	Sample	Population	Sample	Population	Sample	Population	Sample	Population
	Per Cent							
Psychoanalysts	14.0 (103)	16.0 (168)	16.4 (166)	15.7 (241)	16.5 (369)	18.8 (761)	16.0 (638)	17.7 (1170)
Psychiatrists	20.5 (151)[a]	25.1 (264)	21.1 (214)[a]	27.5 (421)	16.4 (368)[a]	22.2 (899)	18.4 (733)[a]	23.9 (1584)
Clinical Psychologists	36.5 (268)	33.0 (347)	41.1 (417)	37.9 (580)	34.8 (780)	31.0 (1256)	36.7 (1465)	32.9 (2183)
Psychiatric Social Workers	29.0 (213)	25.9 (273)	21.4 (217)	18.9 (289)	32.3 (724)	27.9 (1130)	28.9 (1154)	25.5 (1692)
Total	100.0 (735)	100.0 (1052)	100.0 (1014)	100.0 (1531)	100.0 (2241)	99.9 (4046)	100.0 (3990)[b]	100.0 (6629)

[a] Significant at the .05 level. The t ratio was used to test the difference between percentages. (For a discussion of the t ratio see Deming, 1950, p. 314.)

[b] Two respondents refused to designate their professional affiliation.

the largest concentration of medically oriented psychiatrists. Similarly, the difference between Los Angeles and Chicago could be accounted for by the same proposition.

Table 54 also provides a description of the professional composition of the three mental health communities. Looking at the population distributions, we find that New York City has the most uniform distribution of the four professional groups, which is understandable in terms of the variety of training centers in that city. Similarly, the composition of the Los Angeles professional population is consistent with its tendency to recruit personnel from other regions and its high rate of experimentation in psychotherapeutic practices. Specifically, Los Angeles has the largest proportion of clinical psychologists and psychiatrists and the smallest proportion of psychiatric social workers and psychoanalysts. The latter two groups probably tend to be somewhat more traditional in their professional practices, whereas clinical psychologists tend to be the most mobile group and, together with psychiatrists, are probably more likely to be involved in innovative programs.

A more refined assessment of the representativeness of the sample in each metropolitan community was made by comparing the returns and nonreturns by sex, age, major job title, and type of work setting. (Tables showing the distributions of returns and nonreturns by these dimensions are available upon request from William E. Henry, Committee on Human Development, The University of Chicago.) In general the returns accurately reflected the sex composition of the population in each of the communities. However, the proportion of female clinical psychologists and psychiatric social workers in the return group is smaller than the proportion in the nonreturn group, by 4.5 per cent and 8 per cent, respectively. Since females in these two groups were more difficult to locate and are, perhaps, less research oriented than males, these differences were expected. Similarly, with regard to city totals, the proportion of males in the nonreturn group exceeds the proportion in the return group by 4.2 per cent, which reflects the tendency of the male-dominated groups, psychiatry and psychoanalysis, to return at a lower rate than the two groups having more female members. But it seems safe to conclude that the differential sex composition of the population of mental health practitioners in the three metropolitan communities is adequately reflected in the survey returns.

The second factor on which we compared the returns and nonreturns was age. Unfortunately, the comparisons had to be limited to psychoanalysts, psychiatrists, and clinical psychologists, since information on age, job title, and work setting was not available for psychiatric social workers. The findings on age are similar to those on sex in the extent to which the returns and nonreturns have comparable distributions. The only groups with a significantly larger proportion of nonreturns than returns are middle-aged psychiatrists and psychoanalysts—in both cases by about 8 per cent. Thus, in terms of totals, we had less success in getting returns from practitioners over 50 years of age than from younger professionals. However, in none of the comparisons does the distribution of returns grossly underrepresent the population distribution.

In addition to comparisons on the general characteristics of age and sex, it was also possible to make more specific comparisons of returns and nonreturns by examining the job titles that members of the total population listed in their autobiographical sketches in the professional directories. (Both the American Psychiatric Association and the American Psychological Association directories indicate all professional positions currently held by their members.) The representativeness of the survey returns was clearly revealed when the three professions were examined. These job titles were classified into the same nine categories for each of the three professions. Of these thirty-six comparisons, there were only six in which the proportion of nonreturns exceeded the proportion of returns by 1 per cent. The most notable difference was found in the distribution of *total* returns and nonreturns for private practitioners. A larger proportion (by 3.3 per cent) of professionals in the nonreturn category listed private practice as a job title than was true for professionals in the return category. The striking element about this pattern is that there is no significant difference between return and nonreturn private practitioners within any of the professions in any of the metropolitan communities. In fact, the difference between returns and nonreturns is about the same for all three professions, with the proportion of returns always slightly smaller than nonreturns. The differences in total returns and nonreturns apparently reflect the distinction between solo and institutionally affiliated practitioners rather than medical/nonmedical professional differences. The explanation for the lower return rate of private practitioners would therefore seem to revolve around their lack of interest in research, particularly survey research.

The final basis for comparing the returns with the nonreturns is according to the types of work settings the practitioners listed in the professional directories. Of all the population characteristics discussed, type of work setting is undoubtedly more strongly related to the behavior of these professionals than any of the others (Spray, 1968). It is for this reason that the strong similarity we found in the distribution of returns and nonreturns among the categories of work setting provides strong assurance that the sample is generally representative of the population. However, the importance of work setting also dictates that the specific differences that were found between returns and refusals should be carefully noted.

As expected, the most notable difference in return rates by setting is in the category of private practice. Here, as in the case of job title, the significant difference is confined to the total sample (returns = 30.8 per cent, nonreturns = 33 per cent). Similarly, the tendency for the nonreturn category to be larger than the return category holds for two of the three professions. The plausibility of the explanation offered to account for the reluctance of professionals listing private practice as a job title to return the questionnaire is strengthened by this additional evidence on work setting. Specifically, these two sets of findings indicate that solo practitioners are unique in their unwillingness to participate in the research. To a certain extent this unwillingness may stem from their limited professional contacts and lack of interest in research of this type. It may also stem from the fact that they work longer hours and have more patients than other professionals.

The second setting having a larger proportion of nonreturns than returns is that of general hospitals (returns = 13.2 per cent, nonreturns = 17.8 per cent). Since these differences are largely confined to medical professionals, it seems likely that the refusals are either hospital psychiatrists or psychoanalysts in administrative positions. The former group undoubtedly contains many practitioners who adhere to a medical or organic approach to mental illness, which would result in their being antagonistic to the type of research represented by the questionnaire. For psychoanalysts it seems likely that refusals were based less on ideological grounds and more on the basis of situational determinants, such as lack of time or inability of the research staff to contact them. The fact that the difficulty in getting professionals in general hospitals to return the questionnaire was largely confined to New York City tends to support both these contentions.

In assessing the quality of data gathered by the questionnaire survey, we have emphasized the statistical characteristics of the sample of returns. However, there are several relatively unique characteristics of the study that should also be considered in any assessment of the quality of the data. First, the survey was conducted on the total population, rather than a sample, of mental health professionals in three metropolitan communities. Inferences from the relatively high returns can therefore be made to the total population of practitioners with a high degree of confidence. Second, the return rates from each of the professions in the three communities included in the study compares favorably with the rates achieved by other surveys of comparable populations in the mental health field (Kissinger and Tolor, 1964; Strauss et al., 1964; Sundland and Barker, 1962). This is true in spite of the fact that the study included all four high-prestige professions in the mental health field and used an intensive questionnaire requiring more than one hour to complete. Given these considerations, we are led to conclude that the overall quality of the data is high and that generalizations to the professional population in each of the cities can safely be made from findings drawn from the sample of returns. However, there is no basis for drawing conclusions either about all metropolitan communities or about all mental health practitioners. All generalizations about the mental health professions are intended to pertain only to Chicago, Los Angeles, and New York City and should be evaluated from this perspective.

References

American Psychological Association Directory. Washington, D.C.: The American Psychological Association, Inc., 1964.

BACK, K. W., et al. "Public Health as a Career in Medicine." *American Sociological Review,* 1958, *23*(5).

BARRON, F. *Creative Person and Creative Process.* New York: Holt, 1969.

BECKER, H. S., and CARPER, J. W. "The Development of Identification with an Occupation." *American Journal of Sociology,* 1956, *61.*

BECKER, H. S., and GEER, B. "The Fate of Idealism in Medical School." *American Sociological Review,* 1958, *23.*

Biographical Directory of Fellows and Members of the American Psychiatric Association. New York: Bowker, 1963.

BLAIN, D. "Private Practice in Psychiatry." *The Annals of the American Academy of Political and Social Science,* 1953, *286.*

BLAU, P. M., et al. "Occupational Choice, Participation and Social Mobility." *Industrial and Labor Relations Review,* 1956, *9.*

BLUM, A. F., and ROSENBERG, L. "Some Problems Involved in Professionalizing Social Interaction: The Case of Psychotherapy Training." *Journal of Health and Social Behavior,* 1968, *9*(1).

BOGUE, D. J. *The Structure of the Metropolitan Community.* Ann Arbor: University of Michigan Press, 1950.

BUCHER, R., and STRAUSS, A. "Professions in Process." *American Journal of Sociology,* 1961, *66.*

DEMING, W. E. *Some Theory of Sampling.* New York: Wiley, 1950.

Directory of Professional Social Workers. New York: National Association of Social Workers, 1966.

Directory of Social and Health Agencies of New York City 1965–66. New York: Columbia University Press, 1965.

FAUMAN, J. "Occupational Selection Among Detroit Area Jews." In M. Sklare (Ed.), *The Jews.* Glencoe, Ill.: Free Press, 1958.

FOX, R. "Training for Uncertainty." In R. K. Merton, G. G. Reader, and P. Kendall (Eds.), *The Student Physician.* Cambridge, Mass.: Harvard University Press, 1957.

GINZBERG, E., et al. *Occupational Choice.* New York: Columbia University Press, 1951.

GLAZER, N. "The American Jew and the Attainment of Middle Class Rank: Some Trends and Explanations." In M. Sklare (Ed.), *The Jews.* Glencoe, Ill.: Free Press, 1958.

GLAZER, N., and MOYNIHAN, D. P. *Beyond the Melting Pot.* Cambridge, Mass.: M.I.T. Press, 1963.

GOLDBERG, J. "Jews in the Medical Profession—A National Survey." *Jewish Social Studies,* 1939, *1.*

GOODE, W. J. "Community Within a Community: The Professions." *American Sociological Review,* 1957, *22.*

GRAS, N. S. B. *An Introduction to Economic History.* New York: Harper, 1922.

HODGE, R. W., SIEGEL, P. M., and ROSSI, P. "Occupational Prestige in the United States, 1925–63." *The American Journal of Sociology,* 1964, *70*(3).

HOLLINGSHEAD, A. B., and REDLICH, F. C. *Social Class and Mental Illness: A Community Study.* New York: Wiley, 1958.

HOLT, R., and LUBORSKY, L. *Personality Patterns of Psychiatrists.* New York: Basic Books, 1958.

HUGHES, E. "The Making of a Physician." *Human Organization,* 1955, *14.*

KESSEL, R. "Price Discrimination in Medicine." *Journal of Law and Economics,* 1958, *10.*

KISSINGER, R., and TOLOR, A. "The Attitudes of Psychotherapists Toward Psychotherapeutic Knowledge: A Study of Differences Among the Professions." *Journal of Nervous and Mental Disorder,* 1964, *140*(1).

KLERMAN, G., et al. "Sociopsychological Characteristics of Resident Psychiatrists and Their Use of Drug Therapy." *American Journal of Psychology,* 1960, *117*(2).

LENSKI, G. *The Religious Factor.* Garden City, N.Y.: Anchor-Doubleday, 1961.

LEVINSON, D. J. "Medical Education and the Theory of Adult Socialization." *Journal of Health and Social Behavior,* 1967, *8.*

LEWIN, B., and ROSS, H. *Psychoanalytic Education in the United States.* New York: Norton, 1960.

LIVINGSTON, P., and ZIMET, C. "Death-Anxiety, Authoritarianism and Choice of Specialty in Medical Students." *Journal of Nervous and Mental Diseases,* 1965, *140.*

MC KENZIE, R. D. *The Metropolitan Community.* New York: McGraw-Hill, 1933.

MEYER, G. R. "Conflict and Harmony in Nursing Values." *Nursing Outlook,* 1959, *7.*

POPE, L. "Religion and the Class Structure." In R. Bendix and S. M. Lipset (Eds.), *Class, Status and Power: A Reader in Social Stratification.* New York: Free Press, 1966.

RETTIG, S., JACOBSON, F., and PANAMANICK, B. "The Status of the Professional as Perceived by Himself and by Lay Persons." *Mid-West Sociologist,* 1958, *20*(2).

ROSENBERG, M. *Occupations and Values.* Glencoe, Ill.: Free Press, 1957.

RUESCH, J. "Social Factors in Therapy." *Psychiatric Treatment,* Proceedings of the Association of Nervous and Mental Diseases, Vol. 31. Baltimore: Williams and Wilkins, 1953.

RUSHING, W. A. *The Psychiatric Profession: Power, Conflict, and Adaptation in a Psychiatric Hospital Staff.* Chapel Hill: University of North Carolina Press, 1964.

SEWELL, W. H., HALLER, O., and PORTES, A. "The Educational and Early Occupational Attainment Process." *American Sociological Review,* 1969, *34*(1).

SHAPIRO, A. L. "Racial Discrimination in Medicine." *Jewish Social Studies,* 1948, *10.*

SIMPSON, I. H. "Patterns of Socialization into Professions: The Case of Student Nurses." *Sociological Inquiry,* 1967, *37.*

SPRAY, S. L. "Mental Health Professions and the Division of Labor in a Metropolitan Community." *Psychiatry: Journal for the Study of Interpersonal Processes,* 1968, *31*(1).

SROLE, L., et al. *Mental Health in the Metropolis: The Midtown Manhattan Study.* New York: McGraw-Hill, 1962.

STRAUSS, A., et al. *Psychiatric Ideologies and Institutions.* New York: Free Press, 1964.

STRODBECK, F., MC DONALD, M., and ROSEN, B. "Evaluation of Occupations: A Reflection of Jewish and Italian Mobility Differences." *American Sociological Review,* 1957, *22*(5).

SUNDLAND, D. M., and BARKER, E. N. "The Orientations of Psychotherapists." *Journal of Consulting Psychology,* 1962, *26.*

SUPER, D. "A Theory of Vocational Development." *American Psychologist,* 1953, *8.*

SUPER, D., and BACHRACH, P. B. *Scientific Careers and Vocational Development Theory.* New York: Columbia University, Teachers College, Bureau of Publications, 1957.

UNDERHILL, R. "Values and Post-College Career Change." *The American Journal of Sociology,* 1966, *72*(2).

U. S. Bureau of the Census. "Religion Reported by the Civilian Population of the United States, March, 1957." *Current Population Reports: Population Characteristics,* Series P-20, No. 79, February 1958.

VEROFF, J., FIELD, S., and GURIN, G. "Achievement Motivation and Religious Background." *American Sociological Review,* 1962, *27*(2).

WILENSKY, H. L. "The Professionalization of Everyone?" *American Journal of Sociology,* 1964, *70*(2).

ZANDER, A., COHEN, A., and STOTLAND, E. *Role Relations in the Mental Health Professions.* Ann Arbor: University of Michigan Research Center for Group Dynamics, Institute for Social Research, 1957.

Index

C

E

F

G

H

I

J

K

L

M

O

P